Making Rustic Originals

Turning Furniture Finds Into Folk Art

ABBY RUOFF

Hartley & Marks
PUBLISHERS

Published by

HARTLEY & MARKS PUBLISHERS INC.

P. O. Box 147   3661 West Broadway
Point Roberts, WA   Vancouver, WA
98281   V6R 2B8

LIBRARY OF CONGRESS CATALOGING-IN-PUBLICATION DATA

Ruoff, Abby.
     Making rustic originals : turning furniture finds
         into folk art / by Abby Ruoff.
         p.   cm.
     Includes index.
     ISBN 0-88179-155-5

     1. Rustic woodwork.   2. Country furniture.   3. Used furniture.
     4. Decoration and ornament, Rustic.   I. Title.
   TT200.R7797   1998
   684'.0028'8—dc21   98-35415
                                                 CIP

Design & Composition by Hartley & Marks Publishers Inc.

Set in WALBAUM, EXPONTO and SCALA SANS

Printed in Hongkong

To my daughters, Jessica and Rebecca,
For all the fun and laughter, past and present.

*A*lso by Abby Ruoff

Making Twig Furniture & Household Things
Making Twig Garden Furniture
Weddings with More Love Than Money

$\mathcal{A}$CKNOWLEDGMENTS

A special thank you to all who helped with this book: to my publisher, Vic Marks, for all his confidence and assistance, his skill in the art of fine tuning and all the good laughs we've shared; to my editor, Susan Juby, for her infallible advice and editorial skills, her gentle good nature and wonderful sense of humor; to my friend Joyce Grant, of the Phoenicia Antique Center, for her energy and wit, along with the inspirational finds she has uncovered for me; to Irwin Post, for his interest in my work, his advice and expertise in the art of applied birchbark; with admiration to Edward R. Turner, for his ability to bring my designs to life with his sensitive drawings; to my good friend Jim Williams, creative designer and stylist extraordinaire, who volunteered to help direct the photography, and to master photographer Michael Watson—kudos to both of you for your many good ideas, and for remaining cheerful through a marathon photo session.

And to my husband Carl, my anchor, without whose help this book would have taken much longer to complete, who has packed and carried a plethora of shabby treasures home for me, and continues to keep his sense of humor through it all, thank you!

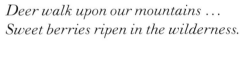

Deer walk upon our mountains …
Sweet berries ripen in the wilderness.

—Wallace Stevens, "Sunday Morning"

CONTENTS

$\mathcal{P}$ART TWO:

Folk Art for Rustic Revisions

$\mathcal{P}$ART THREE:

Rustic Style Faux Finishes

$\mathcal{P}$ART FOUR:

Recycling to Achieve the Rustic Camp Look

$\mathcal{I}$NTRODUCTION

$\mathcal{M}$y adventures with revamping yard sale finds goes back to when we were furnishing our first home. In decorating magazines and trendy shops I would see items that I could have made myself by fixing up furniture I had discovered for next to nothing at garage sales. I became a dedicated revamper early on. I found that a little imagination went a long way toward renewing and recycling garage sale finds. Never one to leave a bargain behind, I began to collect items for future projects. A discarded wagon wheel hub and pottery jugs became table lamps, a garden gate became a guest room headboard, an iron sewing machine base supported our kitchen table, and dollar chairs were re-upholstered with vintage rugs.

Garage sales came of age in the early sixties when the term "garage sale" first appeared in *Webster's Dictionary*. Before the 1950s middle-class people shied away from anything resembling a house sale. Such events were likened to "rummage sales" or the British "jumble sales," which consisted of donated items offered at low cost to the needy in church basements. People have been collecting fine antiques for centuries, but it was not until 1953 that the word "collectible" was introduced to the English language to explain objects amassed outside the realm of traditional paintings, stamps, coins and certified antiques. Collectibles generally refers to items mass-produced from 1945 to 1980 and can include anything from advertising buttons to lunch kits. Nostalgia hunters have helped to popularize garage sales and propel them into the realm of acceptable shopping. Because most collectibles are worth more in their original condition, you will not want to do anything to alter their appearance or detract from their value. There are more than enough nondescript objects available at yard sales for revamping, so stick to those and leave the collectibles to the collectors.

Today's best-dressed houses often include tag sale treasures and owners who actually boast about the low prices of the individual pieces, despite the fact that they can well afford premium antiques. Decorating with secondhand finds is definitely *de rigeur.* It always amazes me that no matter how many garage sales I visit, I often discover some unique item I have never encountered before, such as the little black clips that helped make the simple picture frame found on page 46, or the wonderful star-embossed brass carpet corners used to trim another frame, found on page 50. I once found a funny little pedestal at a church lawn sale, which you can see on page 115. It is such a useful item for holding up a plant or a cake plate or a salad bowl that won't fit on the buffet table, that I wish I could find another one like it. These one-of-a-kind objects with their humble origins help to add warmth and personality to a room. You will often see savvy collectors and bargain hunters, as well as decorators and dealers, shopping shoulder to shoulder in search of treasures at a Saturday morning sale.

When I began creating rustic twig furniture I was often called upon to create quick and easy rustic pieces for home decorating magazines. I found that by adding bark and twigs to my ready supply of garage sale treasures I was able to find even more new uses for old items, and my career as a rustic craft designer flourished. The trend toward personalized decorating encourages people to take neglected or abandoned items and turn them into works of art. When you start thinking about how an object that catches your eye might be saved, you will be amazed how many creative ideas you can come up with. You will certainly never look at a rusty old tin bucket the same way after you see one turned into a lampshade (see page 92).

Years ago I spent countless hours stripping and refinishing furniture to furnish our houses. Today's move toward worn and painted finishes has liberated me and I have sworn I will never strip again! Because authentic antique painted pieces are increasingly expensive and hard to find, I now receive many requests from clients and magazine editors who want "instant folk art." I have developed a collection of simple techniques using water-based paints that mimic folk art. Using these techniques I am often able to complete a piece in a few hours, compared to the week or two required for more traditional techniques using oil-based paints. Fanciful finishes can transform even the most ordinary item into an extraordinary one, and will help to add visual excitement to any room. Modern paints and materials allow even the most reluctant do-it-yourselfer to become an artist.

Sales, Sales, Sales

TAG, ESTATE & MOVING SALES

You never know what marvelous item you are going to turn up among the dusty odds and ends at a tag sale. Hunting for that special item is as much a part of the fun for bargain seekers as finding it. Tag sale aficionados can be categorized into two basic types. There are those in quest of stylish items and those out for a bargain. Most people fit into both categories. Tag sales are a great place to unearth furniture finds, because almost no one is interested in those broken dishes and empty TV cabinets but you. Most of the shoppers are seeking Fiesta Ware, McCoy cookie jars and the latest fad items.

Tag sales are generally held Friday through Sunday, and advertised in the classified section of the local newspaper starting on Wednesday. Well-organized shoppers plan their route according to the advertisements. Holiday weekends in the summer are a prime time for sales and the major players are out at dawn. Hours are usually posted in the advertisements, but ordinary rules of etiquette seem to be lost on serious tag sale shoppers. "No early birds" is a common phrase used to discourage the pre-dawn, flashlight-in-hand crowd, but it doesn't always work. I've seen advertisements that state "Early birds will be shot!" in a futile effort to hold off the hordes of bargain-hungry hunters. Others invite mayhem with "Early birds welcome!" Fortunately, revampers do not have to compete with the really serious tag sale shoppers. There is almost always an adequate supply of one-armed chairs and dusty lampshades that remain unsold at the end of the day. Everyone ends up happy at these sales. The seller is delighted to make money from unwanted clutter, and at the same time, the buyers are thrilled with their finds.

Educate yourself by regularly reading the advertisements for sales. Learn to recognize professional sales, which are sometimes advertised as "estate sales" and usually run by experts. This is not to say that these sales cannot yield big payoffs. Treasures at bargain prices can be found beyond the stacks of Wedgewood and Waterford if you know where to look. If permitted, always check the basement and garage, as well as any outbuildings, at estate sales. Dusty objects just waiting for reuse and reinterpretation often lurk in out-of-the-way places. I once found a handmade wooden rake for fifty cents in a chicken coop that later became a hat rack in a ski cabin.

Moving sales often yield great finds because the owners are frequently moving to smaller quarters. Get to know the neighborhoods near you. Sales at houses built in the late fifties and early sixties are often held by retirees and empty-nesters who are clearing out almost fifty years of accumulated belongings. Everyone knows that sales at old farm houses can yield a bonanza for bargain hunters, but the competition is sometimes daunting at such sales. You might be better off heading in the opposite direction, for a sale that is less well attended. Sometimes the most unassuming houses contain the best finds. Not all sales are advertised in the newspaper, so be on the lookout for signs posted in the neighborhood. Some of these signs, however, may be for permanent sales that remain set up for an entire season, to which new merchandise is only rarely added.

Garage Sale/Flea Market Essentials

*H*ere are a few things experienced sale aficionados never go without: comfortable shoes; a local road map; a magnifying glass, a tape measure; a flashlight (if you plan to arrive early); sunglasses and sunscreen lotion; $1.00 and $2.00 bills (low denominations are always appreciated); a checkbook; disposable, premoistened hand-wipes (handy for cleaning your hands after rummaging through dusty items); and last, but not least, a waist pack or multi-pocketed vest to carry these items.

*A*lthough tag sales and garage sales are relatively new, an innovation of the latter half of the twentieth century, flea markets and auctions have been around for a long time. The "flea market" gets its name from the Parisian Marche aux Puces, an open-air market in Paris where bug-infested furniture was sold. The *Marche aux Puces* is still going strong today and permanent and weekend flea markets dot the landscape in small towns and major cities throughout the United States and Canada. Some are very small affairs with only a handful of dealers set up along a roadside. Some major markets are housed indoors in empty warehouses or parking garages. Others, like the Twenty-Sixth Street Weekend Flea Market in Manhattan, are held outdoors year-round in vacant parking lots. There are a few granddaddy sales across the country such as the Brimfield Shows in Massachusetts; Renninger's in Kutztown, Pennsylvania; The Kane County Market, forty miles outside Chicago; First Monday Trade Days in Canton, Texas; and the famous Los Angeles area Rose Bowl Market. In Canada, there are also several permanent markets. In British Columbia, there is the Abbotsford Flea Market and the HiWay 10 Flea Market in Surrey. In Ontario, there is the Barrie 400 Market, Toronto's Dr. Flea's Highway 27 and the Albion Flea Market. Quebec has its own Marche aux Puces de Saint Eustache. These are just a few; there is probably a permanent flea market near your community. Weekly flea markets are more casual and leisurely than the annual or semi-annual variety. For these, deal-

FLEA
MARKETS

ers line up in the dark, waiting for the gates to open. These sales often resemble an Olympic event for the strong and able-bodied.

Many a flea market item originated at a tag sale, so keep that in mind when considering how much you are willing to pay for an item. Set a price in your mind that seems reasonable before you ask "How much?" and walk away if the dealer quotes you a figure that is way out of line. There are polite ways to ask for a price reduction, and common courtesy suggests that you ought to refrain from saying you saw it cheaper somewhere else. Also, no one wants to hear that your grandmother threw away an item just like the one you are interested in. After all, the reason that such items are scarce and desirable is that so many people threw them away. Try asking, "Can you do better on this?" or "Is this your lowest price?" Dealers price things with reduction in mind and you can usually expect to get ten percent off the marked price.

Sometimes, the higher the ticket price the greater the discount the dealer is willing to give. For items over a hundred dollars, some dealers will lower their price by fifteen or twenty percent. Great buys can also be found at the end of the day when dealers are closing up and don't want to have to pack up the leftover items again. If you are interested in several items from one dealer ask for a price for the whole lot. Many dealers are willing to lower their prices to rock bottom if you are buying in quantity. Some dealers accept checks, but most prefer cash. Out-of-town checks are definitely out.

AUCTIONS   *A*s well as being entertaining and social, auctions often yield marvelous finds. If you are a novice to auctions, try to attend a few without bidding, to get an idea of how they work. The auctioneer's rhythmic chant may take some getting used to as it can be quite hypnotic and even seasoned auction-goers sometimes get lost in the bidding. Don't be intimidated by the fast pace of the auctioneer's banter, nor fearful that if you scratch your nose you will end up the proud owner of that $100,000 Fabergé egg on the auction block. Most auctioneers rely on eye contact and can tell the difference between a scratch and a bid.

When you arrive at the auction you will need to register with the cashier, who will give you a bidding paddle. The paddle may be a permanent wooden paddle or simply a throw-away paper plate with a number on it. There may be a charge for the paddle which will be deducted from your purchases or paid up front and returned to you when you hand in your number. Make sure to ask the cashier what the payment policies are and carefully read all the signs around the cashier's area. Be on the lookout for a 10% Buyer's Premium, which is a percentage tacked on to your actual purchase price. It is easy to forget this added expense during the excitement of the bidding.

All auctions permit viewing several hours before the bidding begins to allow you to view the items that will be coming up for sale. Look at things very carefully, turn them over and beware of repairs. Strict Buyer Beware, As Is and No Returns rules usually prevail. If you wind up with a ripped painting or a cracked vase, I'm afraid it's yours to keep.

On-site auctions are common in small towns and villages when households are being disbanded. On-site auctions often contain a lifetime's supply of memorabilia and goods, and sometimes the accumulation of several generations. These auctions are usually advertised in local papers, sometimes under Farm Dispersal, Farms for Sale or Auctions. Entire households may be moved indoors to a grange hall, a church hall or an auction barn for the sale. Many auction barns hold weekly sales. Auction barn sales usually attract a lot of local regulars week after week, whose bidding number and reserved seat never changes. The benefit auction is another type of auction commonly held in country towns. Items are donated to the benefit auction to help raise money for nonprofit organizations, such as churches, libraries or service clubs. The auctioneer's services are volunteered and the atmosphere tends to be communal and friendly. If you attend one of these auctions you are sure to be inspired to revamp some item. People look with fresh eyes on their neighbor's donation, and almost everyone carries something home.

If you think of auctions as live theatre with audience participation you will almost certainly have a great experience, and for the incurable recycler, there is the added bonus of the possibility of coming across a "find" which, as we will see in the following sections, is anything that can be revamped and made into an innovative piece of rustic camp furniture using a variety of simple techniques.

HOW TO
ACHIEVE
THE
RUSTIC CAMP
LOOK

"*T*here is a cottage camp in New England every room of which has been largely furnished by the handiwork of a daughter who has learned to use tools, and at a cost almost too small to be reckoned. Her materials were boxes, barrels, and pieces of pine boards."

So wrote Frank DuPoy in his 1900 *New Century Home Book*. The rustic simplicity described above is as admired today as it was at the turn of the last century. Our homes are the perfect place to surround ourselves with gently worn objects that reveal a bit about our history and our values. The things that fill our homes can tell the stories of our lives, even if they only reflect the ways we wish our lives had been. Our household items are truly the stuff that dreams are made of. We want our homes to suggest those sweet childhood summers of long ago, whether real or imagined. Most of us wish we grew up on Walden Pond, perhaps because so many of us are sick and tired of escalating prices and modern-day wastefulness, and fed up with a pace of life that whips over us like a New England blizzard. The camp look hearkens back to a simpler time. It allows us the freedom to take the old and make it new again.

Camp style is fun and celebrates the rich heritage of our national culture. It encompasses natural twig and bark embellished furnishings, along with various forms of folk art. Faux finishes, designed with Yankee ingenuity to imitate more costly materials, helped to shape this fundamental American style. Time-honored craft techniques applied in new and exciting ways help fit the rustic camp look into everyday surroundings. No longer restricted to a lakeside camp or remote mountain cabin, the rustic camp look is more popular than ever and possible for anyone with a sense of adventure to create.

PART 1

Revamping Using *Rustic Elements*

1

Love Seat

With a Twig Frame

There are surprises at every turn for a bargain hunter. I know I certainly did not expect to find myself watching a man tie a furniture frame on top of my car one autumn afternoon. I had stopped with a friend at an unadvertised neighborhood yard sale on a whim. "I'd like to see you do something with this," she challenged, gesturing at the naked loveseat that sat off to one side. Fifteen dollars seemed like a reasonable price

and I can't resist a dare, so I bought the loveseat. I was almost certain I could figure out a way to bring it back to life without spending a fortune. Almost as soon as I got it home I thought of adding twigs to its sturdy and well-constructed frame. An armload of pillows helped to turn it into a very comfortable seat and it is where my friend always sits when she comes to visit. Because it is not always easy to find empty frames at sales, you might consider upholstered pieces, which are often sold at give-away prices. Stripping fabric, padding, nails and webbing is time-intensive, but the end results can be very worthwhile.

Tools and Materials

You will need an axe or saw for cutting trees; a ruler or marking pencil; a drill and a selection of bits; clippers or garden shears; a hammer; 1½" galvanized roofing nails, 1½" finishing nails; safety goggles and work gloves. I used willow for this project as it is abundant in my area and I enjoy working with its pliable branches, but any green (fresh) local hardwood such as hickory, beech or birch would be suitable.

METHOD

1. This 57" wide, 30" deep loveseat frame, with its 33" high back, required a selection of ¼" to ¾" diameter branches, 21" to 33" long; 6 branches were used on each side; 12 on the back, and 14 make up the seat.

2. Beginning on one side and working from back to front, position one branch along the arm and gently bend it toward the front along the bottom seat support. Using pilot hole and nail construction, drill and nail the branch in place, referring to the photograph. Repeat with the remaining side branches along both sides. *Note*: To make a pilot hole,

hammer a nail that is smaller than the nail or screw you will be using partway into the object. A pilot hole makes it easier to drive in the actual nail or screw.

3. Position the middle seat support branch along the front and back seat supports, and using pilot hole and nail construction, attach the branch. Continuing from the center and moving outward, attach the remaining seat supports in the same manner.

4. Working on the back of the loveseat, beginning with the center branch and moving outward on both sides, attach the back branches as pictured, using pilot hole and nail construction.

5. If necessary, cut the ends of the branches so they are even.

2

Rocking Chair

With a Twig Seat & Back

Found at a yard sale, this timeworn treasure takes on new life with a simple twig-stringing technique. Once you discover how easy it is to repair chairs with this method, you will be searching for forgotten pieces to turn into tomorrow's heirlooms. Build the jig and adjust the spacing for your particular chair—for the seat only, or for the seat and back as in this project.

Tools and Materials

You will need an axe or saw for cutting twigs; a crosscut handsaw; a ruler; a marking pencil; a drill and a selection of bits; and wire clippers. (Note: The materials listed are for the specific chair illustrated. This antique chair originally had a caned back and seat, and so had pre-drilled holes along the rim surrounding the back and the seat. The threaded twig wires are inserted through the holes.)

You should use wood such as beech, willow, birch or hickory. You will need 32 straight twigs, 15" long and ½" to 1" in diameter for the back; 15 straight twigs, 16" to 21" long and ½" to 1" in diameter for the seat; four straight wires, approximately 30" long and ⅛" in diameter; two pieces of board approximately 21" long to make the jigs; one large nail to use with the jigs; and two forked twigs, 1" in diameter for the arms. (*Note:* The length of the seat twigs will vary to accommodate the shape of the seat, while the back opening is uniform).

METHOD

1. Cut 32 twigs, 15" long and ½" to 1" in diameter for the back.
2. Cut 15 twigs 16" to 21" long with diameters from ½" to 1" for the seat.

Making the Jig

1. One board can be used to make a jig for both the seat and the back (Figure 2-1). For the back, drill two holes 14" apart in a straight board that is at least 21" long. For the seat, drill two holes 17" apart in a straight board that is at least 21" long.

Drilling the Twigs

1. In the 32 twigs for the back, drill holes 14" apart. Your drill bit size should be just slightly larger than

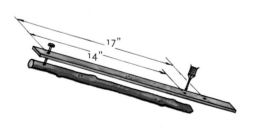

FIG. 2-1

the ⅛" thickness of your wire. Center them using the
jig as a guide (Figure 2-1). (*Note:* To drill the second
hole in each twig, place the nail in the first drilled
hole through the jig into the branch. This holds the
jig in place and ensures accuracy.)

2. In the 15 twigs for the seat, drill holes 17" apart using
    the jig as your guide (Figure 2-1).

Arranging the Back

1. Cut two straight wires the length of the back of your
    chair plus 10 extra inches to allow for attaching the 32
    back twigs to the chair.

2. String the 32 drilled twigs onto the two straight
    pieces of wire. Place the first twig in the middle
    of both wires. Continue stringing from both
    directions equally, until all 32 twigs are on the wires
    (Figure 2-2). There should be approximately 5" to 10"
    of wire at the end of the threaded twigs.

3. Bend the bare wire at each end of the threaded twigs
    and insert the wires through the holes on the back
    outer rim of the chair at the top, and at the bottom of
    the back opening. To secure the wire end, form a
    knot, or hammer a nail partway on the back of the
    chair (near the wire end) and wrap the wire tightly
    around the nail. Using wire clippers, cut the ends of
    the wires.

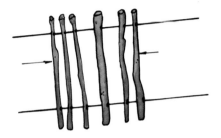

FIG. 2-2

Arranging the Seat

1. Cut two straight wires the length of the seat plus 10
    extra inches to allow for attaching the 15 seat twigs to
    the chair.

2. String the 15 drilled twigs onto the two straight
    pieces of wire. Follow the shape of the seat when
    stringing the seat branches, allowing for slight
    curves.

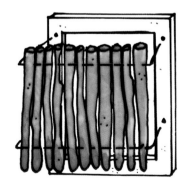

FIG. 2-3

3. Bend the bare wire at each end of the threaded twigs, and insert the wires through the seat rim chair holes at the front, and at the back of the seat opening. Secure the wire ends in the same manner as for the chair back.

Adding the Arms

1. The one-piece forked twig that makes up the arm is attached using pilot hole and nail construction to the chair back at a convenient location, approximately 9" up from the seat at the back; and to the seat side-front.

3

One-Drawer Stand

With Twig Drawer & Antiquing

This was a really dreary little pine stand with a missing drawer and $5 scribbled on it in black crayon. It did not come from a proud old house. Instead it sat at the bottom of the driveway on the side of the road beside a few old chairs, some chipped dishes and several wonderful bushels of tomatoes, squash and corn. There was a sign at the untended sale explaining how to pay and make change. I placed eight dollars and fifty cents in the box for the stand and some vegetables.

Tools and Materials

The drawer is constructed out of ¾" pine for the sides and ¼" pine for the bottom. A table saw is needed to create the straight grooves that support the drawer bottom. Most local lumber yards are equipped to provide table saw work for a nominal charge. You will probably need to use a wood plane to bevel the edges on the drawer bottom to fit it into the grooves. A hand saw is needed to cut the drawer bottom and to split the log. Wood glue and pipe clamps are used to assemble the drawer.

Two angle brackets, requiring six wood screws and a screwdriver, are used to attach the split log front. A 1" to 1½" log is used for the drawer front, extending approximately 2" on each side, beyond the actual drawer. The pull is a 7" long, ½" diameter willow twig simply nailed to the two protruding branch stubs. Consider trying to find a similar log when searching for a drawer front as the stubs make it easy to attach the pull.

Antiquing Materials

You will need a 2" paintbrush; a natural sea sponge; a wire brush; sandpaper; latex paint in white, sage green, and slate gray; a "dirty water glaze" made up of equal parts red and black paint mixed with double the amount of water; and acrylic sealer.

Building the Drawer

1. Measure the inside dimension of the stand to obtain the depth and width required to construct the drawer.
2. One piece of ¾" pine (the total measurement of the width plus depth) is used to construct the sides (depth) and back (width) of the drawer.
3. The groove is cut along the entire piece of the ¾" pine, and the side and back pieces are cut to size after

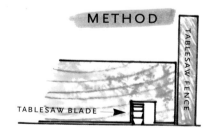

METHOD

TABLESAW FENCE

TABLESAW BLADE

FIG. 3-1

the groove is cut. Using two pieces on a table saw (Figure 3-1), cut a groove ¼" wide, ¼" deep, and ¼" up from the bottom edge of the pine board. (*Note:* Because many home workshops don't have a table saw, this step can be completed at some lumber yards.)

4. After the groove is cut, cut the three lengths (two sides and one back) to size.
5. Assemble the three lengths in place on the worktable to determine the size required for the drawer bottom.
6. To make the drawer bottom, cut a piece of ¼" pine to size.
7. Three edges of the bottom, the two sides and the back, have to be tapered to fit into the grooves. Using a belt sander or sandpaper on a block of wood, sand the three drawer bottom edges to slightly less than ¼", making sure that the edges still fit into the grooves.
8. Use wood glue along the drawer edges and insert the edges in the grooves, using pipe clamps to hold them fast until they dry. (*Note:* Types of glue and temperature can vary drying time. See glue manufacturer's specifications for drying time.)
9. Remove the pipe clamps and attach the split log front with two angle brackets.
10. Attach the twig pull to the drawer using two finishing nails.

Antiquing the Stand

After I built the drawer and faced it with a split white birch log, the stand needed some form of antiquing to make the piece cohesive. The technique for producing a distressed paint look varies from piece to piece. Antiquing refers to any technique that makes a piece appear naturally aged, from the rich patina of a well-cared-for

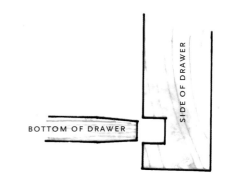

BOTTOM OF DRAWER   SIDE OF DRAWER

FIG. 3-2

FIG. 3-3

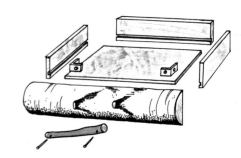

FIG. 3-4

heirloom to the neglected objects found in dusty barns and chicken coops.

One technique involves applying a thinned wash of acrylic burnt umber, gray or black all over the piece with a damp sea sponge or a soft rag, leaving it to dry for a moment, and then rubbing it with a lintless rag (such as an old T-shirt) to wipe off the excess. By exerting a bit more pressure in areas that would naturally be more worn, highlights and shading are created. Then rub a thin coat of beeswax polish (or any good-quality paste furniture polish) over the entire piece. Finally, use a heavy hand and a soft cloth to rub the waxed finish to achieve a transparent sheen. By applying additional coats of wax and buffing again, you will end up with the mellowed look of a cherished antique.

Another antiquing technique (also not used here) is to paint the base one color, let it dry and rub wax onto the parts that would be naturally aged. Then paint another color on top of the first and let it dry. Then, using fine-grade steel wool, rub back the second coat so that the first coat shows through. Finally, antiquing wax is rubbed into the whole piece with a cloth.

Experiment and learn to trust your judgment regarding how much paint to put on and how much to take off. Think about how things age naturally, and keep this in mind when antiquing. Multiple layers of paint are chipped and nicked through time and dirt and grime collect in the crevices, making the recessed areas deeper. This piece needed a soft rustic look in order to blend in with the birchbark drawer front so I used a simple but effective antiquing technique I developed years ago.

1. I painted everything except the top of the table with a creamy coat of latex the color of daisies.
2. I poured a dollop of sage green and an equal amount of slate gray onto an old dish. I dipped a dry sea sponge onto the surface of the paint and applied dabs of both colors to the table, one at a time. It is not necessary to wait for one color to

dry before adding the second. Take care not to overload your sponge or the antiquing effect will be lost. As with the other techniques discussed here, if you don't like the effect your antiquing produces, wait for the paint to dry and begin again. Experiment with a damp sponge and slightly watered-down paint for a faded effect.

3. After this I used a wire grill brush to remove some of the paint and produce the scratches usually associated with a worn piece.

4. I rubbed sandpaper over the green layer, exposing the white, as well as some of the natural wood.

5. I used a damp sea sponge to apply a "dirty water glaze" with a solution of red and black paint diluted enough to make it almost transparent. I rubbed most of the glaze off, allowing some tinges to penetrate the paint finish, continuing to apply and remove the glaze until I had the effect I wanted. I decided to leave the top surface of the table because it was in good condition.

6. I sealed the entire piece, including the top, with repeated coats of flat acrylic sealer to preserve the finish.

4

Iron Bed Frame

With Refinished Iron & Wattle Weaving

When I bought this charming bed at a country auction for a dollar the auctioneer shouted, "I'll never sell another iron bed again!" Later I was told that these beds never bring more than a dollar or two and often the auction house has to throw them out or collect several to take to the scrap metal yard. This seems sad to me, for I have wonderful memories of similar beds in the summer camps of my childhood. My grandmother had a pair like this

in the little back bedroom of her brown shingled guest cabin. Her beds were painted white and had blue and yellow patchwork quilts as bedspreads. Their sturdy iron frames served generations of sleepers, and if you have an opportunity to buy one of these durable beds I suggest you do. They are now being reproduced and sold to sophisticated urban customers who are trying to re-create the rustic cabin feeling.

Tools and Materials

You will need work gloves; safety goggles; and a wire brush and medium-grade aluminum oxide sandpaper if the wire piece has to be refinished before weaving. You will also need red acrylic enamel paint and a 2" wide brush for a base coat, along with bronze metallic paint for a top coat (optional). The branches needed are described under Weaving, below

Refinishing Iron
(preparing iron and wire for wattle weaving)

METHOD

Any item constructed with a wire or iron framework makes an excellent foundation for wattle or vine weaving. Wire stands and magazine racks from the fifties and sixties with their ready-made "spokes" or "bars" are ideal for weaving supple branches over and under. Small wire items such as egg baskets, milk carriers or canning racks make nice beginner projects, when woven with very thin willow shoots or vines. The wire or iron may need some refinishing if it is rusted or painted an unattractive color. If you are anything like me you will want to get this part over with as quickly as possible in order to get to the fun part—the actual transformation.

If you decide you need to refinish your wire or iron piece before weaving it, you will need a pair of good work gloves, safety goggles and a wire brush to get started. It is best to work outdoors, for little fragments of flying metal can make a mess.

1. Vigorously rub the wire brush (a long-handled grill brush is excellent for this purpose) over the rusted areas, removing the loose bits. It is not necessary to have a smooth finish, for most of the spokes will be covered with wattling, and any coarse texture that may show through is perfectly acceptable and even desirable in some instances.
2. If you want to remove more of an old finish, use a medium grade of aluminum oxide sandpaper first, then rub the piece with the wire brush.

Painting Iron or Wire

Not all wire- or ironware will require painting. Many items are ready for weaving as soon as you get them home from the yard sale.

1. If your wire or iron piece needs painting before you weave with it, begin with a red base coat. Use an exterior acrylic enamel paint and any old 2" wide brush. Hopefully, as with the refinishing, you will be painting your piece outside to cut down on the mess. Red undertones will help to obscure the original finish while adding a hint of authenticity.
2. Allow the undercoat to dry thoroughly for at least three hours.
3. For the top coat use a dark bronze or other metallic finish (available at most hardware stores). The new metallic paints are perfect for restoring old iron and wire pieces and often make them look better than new. Allow the top coat to dry overnight.

Weaving

You will need very supple willow branches for weaving
through the metal bars or the headboard and footboard.
The willow should be from 2" to 6" longer than the piece
they are being woven through so they will stay in place.
Approximately 25 willow shoots were used to weave this
bed. If you live nearby a lush willow and your piece is not
too difficult to move, you may have the luxury of being
able to weave on-site with the freshest, most pliable
shoots available.

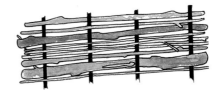

FIG. 4-1

1. Wireware pieces with narrow bars will permit
    traditional under/over weaving.
2. For large items, such as this iron bed, the weaving
    will require a different approach. It may seem as
    though the willow has a mind of its own as it winds
    its way through the spokes of your project. As you
    work the shoots under and over the iron spokes, it
    will become apparent that you have to proceed in a
    random fashion: under two, over two, under three,
    over one. The length, diameter and pliability of the
    branches will help to determine the weave.
3. Vary the rows as you would in conventional basket
    making, alternating the willow placement under or
    over the spokes.

5

Single Magazine Rack

With Wattle Weaving

I think the man who sold me this brass magazine rack (circa 1960) with its silly curved legs and oversized handle felt guilty taking my fifty cents, but I had a vision for it. As soon as I got it home, I sawed off the legs and handle. The classic fan shape, combined with willow weaving, added individuality and style to an instant rustic original.

Tools and Materials

You will need sharp clippers or garden shears; a ruler or measuring tape; safety goggles and work gloves. Almost any metal magazine stand will work, as long as it has spokes you can weave the twigs through. Willow, alder, cottonwood or any other pliable twigs are suitable for weaving. The number of twigs required will depend on the size of the magazine rack frame. For this frame 12" to 23" long twigs were used.

Very supple twigs are woven through the metal spokes. Given the sometimes uncooperative nature of twigs, traditional over and under weaving on every spoke is not always possible. If the wire spokes are close together, the twigs may break if you try to weave them over and under each spoke. Random weaving (as was done in the Project 4: Iron Bed Frame) is best. Try whatever pattern of over/under that keeps the weaving tight and somewhat uniform.

METHOD

FIG. 5-1

6

Record Stand
End Table

With Wattle Weaving

Originally intended to hold a portable phonograph and 33^2 LPs, these wire stands were common in the 1950s, and show up regularly at flea markets and garage sales now that long-play records have given way to CDs. Not everyone, however, has disposed of their vinyl collection and for them, as well as the new breed of record collector, these tables can be very serviceable. The willow weaving and the addition of the two arched ends changes the character of this ordinary stand, producing a very

personal end table, perfect for organizing books, magazines and records.

To make the Record Stand End Table follow the directions for Project 5: Single Magazine Rack With Wattle Weaving. For this project the twigs ranged from 12" to 18" long.

FIG. 5-1

7

Child's Chair

With a Laced Birchbark Seat

This charming example of Mexican folk art was only one dollar, probably because it was missing its seat. A piece of birchbark with its smooth underside placed facing up, a hole punch and a length of rawhide lacing were used to replace the seat. Child-sized chairs make delightful accent pieces, evoking the atmosphere of a much-loved family retreat.

Tools and Materials

This project requires scissors for cutting the birchbark to size; a ruler and marking pencil; a table-model office hole punch; 7½" by 10" piece of peeled birchbark; 130" of rawhide lacing, available at craft shops, sporting goods stores or any place that walking or work boots are sold.

1. Using the ruler and pencil, mark off spaces along the perimeter of the bark, approximately ½" in from the edge and 1" apart.
2. Punch holes at the 1" marks (Figure 7-1).
3. Center the birchbark in the seat space with its smooth underside facing up.
4. Lace the rawhide through the holes.
5. Tie off the rawhide at the back with a square knot and slip the ends under the lacing along the back rail.

Mexican Folk Art

If you aren't lucky enough to find a chair with a motif already on it, use the attached template (Figure 7-2) to apply your own Mexican folk art. Red, white, yellow and blue are usual colors in traditional Mexican art.

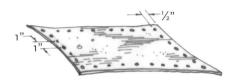

METHOD

FIG. 7-1

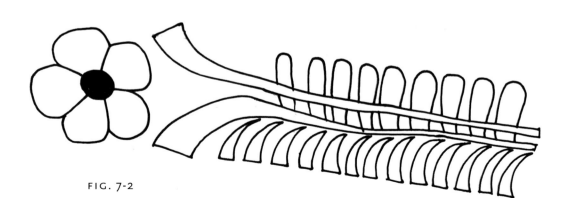

FIG. 7-2

8

PictureFrame

With Clipped Bark Covering

Simple birchbark picture frames, made by early rustic builders and Native American craftspeople, were sold as tourist souvenirs during the early part of the 20th century, and continue to adorn the tabletops and walls of some very fashionable rustic retreats. If you are lucky enough to have an 8" by 10" sheet of pressed birchbark, this easy-to-make frame will add charm to any setting. If you do not have any birchbark on hand, try using a color photocopy of the photo provided on the next page as a

FIG. 8-1

frame or mount for your photo, which can then be covered in glass or framed with another frame (Figure 8-1).

For some reason the odd little black metal clips I used on this frame intrigued me, so I bought them trusting that one day they would come in handy for something, and sure enough, they did. I had a lovely sheet of pressed birchbark on hand and decided to use it to make a simple frame. (See below for how to flatten and dry a sheet of birchbark.) Once a birchbark sheet is dried flat it usually remains flat, so this piece was easy to work with. I marked off the oval opening with a pencil and used sharp scissors to cut it out. The photograph is sandwiched between the bark and an 8" by 10" sheet of thick matte board, all held together with my odd little clips. I have never come across clips like this before and doubt I will again, but I will be on the lookout for items that can be used to clamp things together. Spring-type clothespins (doll size) would work nicely and clip-on earrings would be really "campy."

About Birchbark

*U*se only bark from recently fallen trees. Do not peel bark from living trees. Stripping the bark from live trees will cause the tree to die.

To peel the bark from the branch, score a deep line lengthwise through the bark with a sharp knife. Make two cuts around the branch, marking the section of the bark to be removed.

Place the top of a chisel along the scored line and gently tap it with a mallet. Continue until the section of bark is removed.

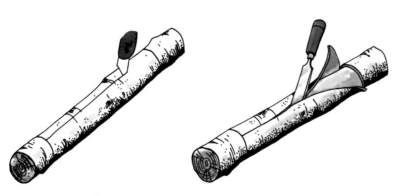

FIG. 8-2   FIG. 8-3

If the project requires pressed bark, press the bark between heavy books or large, flat rocks or bricks until ready to use (Figure 8-4). Depending on where you are comfortable working, pressing bark can be done indoors or outdoors. Although I have successfully peeled bark in all seasons, it is easiest in the spring when the sap is up. To keep bark flexible all you need to do is dampen it with warm water.

FIG. 8-4

9
Bark Strip Frame

With Brass Nail Corners

Now that this five-dollar "garage sale primitive" (see page 51 for an explanation of the term) is framed with crossed strips of birchbark, most people who see it can hardly imagine one without the other. The bark was attached to the frame using brass upholstery nails. Its crossed corners are reminiscent of the antique carved wooden frames that helped decorate Victorian parlors and cabin walls. Star-embossed brass triangles, originally used as carpet corners to help keep runners snug against stairs, provide a decorative embellishment.

Tools and Materials

You will need 4 strips of birchbark, approximately 3" wide, and 4" longer than the frame you are planning to trim; a pencil; a ruler; sharp scissors to cut the bark; and a hammer for attaching the bark strips with brass upholstery nails to the wood frame. Natural materials such as pine cones or seed pods may be used in place of the brass triangles to trim the corners.

METHOD

1. Cut two 3" wide birchbark strips approximately 4" longer than the length of the frame to be covered, and two 3" wide strips approximately 4" longer than the width of the frame.
2. Arrange the strips across the frame with crossed corners, as pictured.
3. Arrange the upholstery nails 1" to 2" apart, and nail in place.
4. Nail the corners in place with some sort of decorative trim. *Note:* If you like the idea of stars, try cutting your own out of scraps of tin or copper sheets.

The Right Art for Bark & Twig Frames

What kinds of art look good in twig or bark frames and suit the rustic camp look? Your options are endless. The pictures can be as simple as a pressed leaf, a calendar picture or a photo of your kids camping in the backyard. If you are looking for tag sale art there are some particular favorites of mine that are consistent with a rustic theme.

To begin, there is the school of art that I like to call "garage sale primitive." Once referred to as Sunday painters, amateur artists produce some charming landscapes, still lifes and portraits, some of which are surprisingly well executed and many of which end up in yard sales. With bark nailed or twigs glued onto the existing frames, these inexpensive paintings will be just the thing to complement your rustic camp style.

In addition, any number of items that turn up at sales may be suitable for framing. A snippet of vintage fabric, old playing cards or canceled stamps pressed under glass can enhance the

simplest room. You will be surprised at how little time it takes to create a masterpiece.

One of the handiest ways I have found to adapt art to rustic frames is to use the full-color photocopying machines that are now available at most print shops. These copiers allow you to make the antique post cards and vintage photographs so abundant at tag sales fit any frame. Look for nature photographs of mountains, lakes and streams, photos of people on picnics, camping, sailing or fishing. Old snapshots with their mellow sepia tints are esthetically pleasing and perfectly at home in a rustic setting. Peruse old catalogs and antique albums for unique pictures. Most of the old photographic images were quite small and using the enlargement feature on a copy machine opens up a world of possibilities. Check the copyright laws for your state or province, but as a general rule, the copyright on anything over 75 years old has expired. Color photocopies usually cost between one and three dollars, depending on the type of paper you choose—a very small price to pay for an original.

FIG. 9-1

10
Mirror Frame

With Bark Refinishing

This pseudo-Chippendale maple mirror has been given a rustic facelift with birchbark. The mirror was in fine condition, but the frame was water-damaged. It was marked $1 at a yard sale, but the woman holding the sale felt so guilty about charging for a damaged item that she gave it to me for nothing. I, in turn, promptly purchased a pair of scissors and some knitting needles, just to be polite. Sometimes you meet the nicest people at sales.

The bark strips are attached to the frame with 1" finishing nails. The tiny nail heads are barely visible, but if they bother you, you can always touch them up with a dab of white paint or white out.

11

Picnic Caddy

With Bark Refinishing

Sometimes the fun isn't in what you find at a sale, but rather in how you use it. I found this wooden shoeshine case at a flea market in Maine one summer and could hardly wait to get it home and recast it. Pieces of birchbark left over from another project were quickly nailed in place around the case and I wrapped a thin sheet of bark around the handle. Filled with rolled napkins and flatware, the picnic caddy is convenient for parties and picnics all year round.

What can you do if you are out of birchbark sheets? Nail or glue on twigs, and wrap the handle with grapevine. Out of twigs? Recycle your carrying case with paint, decoupage or stencils. Whether it is being used for picnics, kitchen utensils or household tools, this little caddy is a blue-ribbon winner.

54

12

Berry Basket

With Rustic Revamping

Farmstands used to give these basic wooden baskets away with your purchase of a pint of fresh berries. Today they are usually recycled, but a friendly greengrocer can often be convinced to include one with your produce. If your large supermarket chain carries only plastic baskets, try asking for a wooden basket at independent markets or small grocery shops. They are becoming more difficult to find, but they can frequently be found at rummage sales in farm communities for a very nominal charge.

The pleasing shape and smooth surface of wooden fruit baskets is a perfect foundation for rustic work. Use a glue gun to attach bits of bark, twigs, mosses, acorns and seed pods and turn your basket into a creative accent for the desk or dressing table. Make several to use as gift containers or use them to hold seed packets. Lined with plastic and planted with kitchen herbs or spring-flowering bulbs, the rustic basket becomes a container garden.

13

Mirror Frame

With Rustic Revamping

Here is a refreshing way to frame a mirror and preserve the memories of a woodland walk. Collecting the materials to make this mirror is almost as much fun as making it.

Tools and Materials

Brown caulking and caulk gun, and a hot glue gun and hot melt adhesive (available at hardware stores and building supply shops) are the only tools required for this easy-to-make project. Gather an assortment of

58

natural materials such as acorns, dried grasses, seeds, fern fronds and bits of fallen bark and mosses. Use packaged Spanish moss (available at craft stores and florist supply houses) to fill in bare areas.

You will need a mirror or picture frame, the wider the better, to show off your collection from the forest floor. The octagonal shape of this multi-surfaced frame helps enhance the natural beauty of the materials, but any wide frame would be attractive. This mirror's gold rim adds luster to the earthen hues around the frame and creates an element of rustic refinement.

METHOD

1. This three-dollar mirror was already painted gold when I bought it. If you want to add a gold edge to your frame, do it with paint or marker before you apply the natural woodland elements.
2. To attach seeds, pods, twigs and grasses to the frame, run a thick bead of brown caulking along the surface of the frame, one section at a time.
3. Arrange and press assorted items into the caulking, adding small pieces of bark and twigs as needed.
4. Repeat for the remaining sections until the frame is completely covered.
5. Subsequent layers are added on top of the first layer in order to hide the caulking. Continue until you are satisfied with the arrangement.
6. Attach the Spanish moss in clumps over any bare spots, using hot melt adhesive and a glue gun.

14

Copper Teapot

With a Wire & Twig Handle

"Everything old is new again," so the saying goes, and that is just what I was thinking when I replaced the missing handle on this chubby copper teapot. A length of coat hanger wire was threaded through the two eyelets, and fashioned into an arc. Three supple willow twigs are twisted and wrapped around the wire to help bring some of the great outdoors home.

Warning: Make sure that any replaced handles on such things as kettles and teapots are securely attached and that the twig or vine elements are clear of any heat sources.

60

15

Walking Stick

With a Hame Handle

The walking stick is a great companion on a hike and adds a charming decorative accent when leaning near your back door, or placed in an umbrella stand on your front porch. Try to find an interesting gnarled and vine-wrapped stick to put your top on.

The horse hames shown here came from an estate sale and were the perfect size and shape to cap off the walking sticks. Hames are the two curved supports attached to the collar of a draft horse, to which the straps of the harness are fastened. Other comfortable and suitable choices to top walking sticks might be drapery rod finials, or drawer knobs.

16.

Umbrella Stand

With Grapevine Weaving

This two-dollar umbrella stand is a good example of a simple rustic makeover. A bundle of grapevine and a few hours of weaving, and you will have created a bit of rustic whimsy to add to your collection.

Weaving with Grapevine

Grapevine is wonderful to work with, but other vines such as peppervine, honeysuckle or Virginia creeper may be substituted. Grapevine grows wild along roadsides and streambeds, but so do the three poison vines: ivy, oak and sumac. There are several plant identification books available to help you learn the difference.

To make your weaving easy gather the vines in the summer, strip them of their leaves, and weave the fresh-cut vines. Vines cut in the fall or winter are brittle and need to be soaked (or boiled) in hot water to make them flexible. This is bound to create a big mess, so I suggest you save your vine-weaving projects for warm weather.

FIG. 16-1

17
Globe Stand

With Three Twig Legs

The thrift store lady who sold me this globe was very apologetic about its missing base, and assured me that she was not responsible for the pricing. She believed that ten dollars was too much to charge for an item with a missing part. I looked at the missing base as a fortuitous opportunity to turn the globe into a hand-crafted original.

The following directions are for a 50" circumference globe and a 24" tall stand. You will have to adjust the measurements to suit your particular globe and stand.

64

Tools and Materials

You will need a crosscut hand saw; garden shears; a sharp pocket knife; a drill with a selection of bits; a pencil; a ruler; a hammer; safety goggles; and work gloves.

Gather three pliable twigs for the legs, such as willow, red dogwood or cedar, approximately 28" long, with diameters of 1" to 2". It is important to select pliable twigs that you can splay out at the bottom. You will also need one hardwood branch, 5" long and 1½" in diameter, for the spacer/globe holder and three 24" long, ½" diameter twigs for the bottom stretchers. Galvanized flathead nails (#4p) fasten the twigs together.

METHOD

1. Begin construction by attaching the legs to the 5" long spacer/globe holder. Butt the spacer against one leg; using the pencil, mark two points 3" apart to join the leg.
2. Drill pilot holes and nail in place.
3. Repeat with the remaining two legs.
4. Place the construction on a work surface. On the inside of each leg make a pencil mark approximately 8" from the bottom. Taper the ends of the bottom stretchers with a sharp pocket knife or garden shears.
5. Butt each stretcher to the leg against which it will be nailed, checking for a tight fit.
6. Drill pilot holes through the ends of the stretchers into 2 legs at the pencil marks.
7. Join the stretcher to the leg, lining up the pilot holes and nailing three-quarters of the way through.
   Note: Leave one quarter of the driven nail exposed until the construction is assembled. This prevents the driven nail from becoming loosened as you proceed.
8. Repeat fitting, drilling and nailing the remaining two stretchers to the two legs, forming an equilateral triangle.

FIG. 17-1

FIG. 17-2

9. Make sure your construction stands straight and even as you proceed. Using a sharp pocket knife or hand saw, trim the legs as necessary to guarantee a straight stand.

10. Attach the globe to the spacer/globe holder using a 1½" screw and metal washer. *Note:* This globe came with a metal rim where it had originally been attached to its missing stand.

18
Banjo Wall Clock

With Bark & Twig Refinishing

Surprisingly, this dusty banjo wall clock was still in working order when I bought it at a church yard sale. Its bottom section held a very dull and faded print, which I replaced with a scrap of birchbark that still had moss attached. A bark panel is tacked onto the body of the clock, and supple willow trims the face and sides. Tiny willow "buttons" cut with garden shears are nailed in place with ½" finishing nails. Decorative and practical, the banjo clock keeps perfect time.

The combination of bark and twigs on a yard sale "special" can create the perfect rustic update. Bark will cover a multitude of sins on flat surfaces and twigs will disguide bent surfaces, leaving you the option of only displaying those parts of the original object that appeal to your eye. One way to think of this kind of update, such as the treatment on the Banjo Wall Clock, is as rustic reupholstering. The bark is like a fabric covering and twigs are a trim, like braid or rope. Combine the two and voila! —an instant and inexpensive classic country accessory is born.

1. If your bark sheets are too small to cover the surface you want to hide, cut several small pieces into squares and glue or nail a patchwork pattern in place.
2. Remember that bark curls as it dries so always press bark pieces under heavy weight when storing.
3. To help flatten small pieces of bark, place a pressing cloth over their undersides and press them with a warm iron.
4. Look for birchbark with lichen or moss growing on it to add a whole new dimension to your projects.
5. Birchbark pieces can easily be sewn together using thread, twine, or raffia and a darning needle.
6. If you are going to paint your project as well as "reupholster" it with bark, always paint first to avoid getting paint on the bark.
7. Deep colors help show off the soft, subtle coloring of bark. Think deep red, forest green, or Shaker blue.
8. A few bark-covered pieces blend in nicely with cabin collectibles such as vintage skiing, boating, and fishing equipment.

Notes on Rustic Reupholstering

*T*o get the reupholstered bark look without bark, make color photocopies of birchbark and using decoupage glue, adhere the colorcopies to your yardsale special. Even tiny snippets of bark can be enlarged and used in this manner. From simple bookcovers to chairs and cupboards, pasted and sealed printed bark paper helps to bring a natural coloring and rustic patterns to a room.

Decoupaging with Bark

19

Horseshoe Lamp

With a Cone-shaped Bark Shade

I transformed this little horse-shoe lamp into a light-hearted accent with a folded cone-shaped piece of birchbark for a shade, secured with two large brass paper fasteners.

Someone went to a great deal of trouble to weld these horse-shoes together to create this original little table lamp. It is an excellent welding job and such a clever use for recycling horse-shoes that I can't help but feel surprised that it ended up selling at an estate sale for only fifty cents.

Purchased lampshades are usually quite expensive and ordinary at best. A laced bark or woven vine shade can be just what a particular lamp needs to evoke that casual rustic cabin look. When deciding on a shade, be brave and allow your playful spirit to take over. Remember, revamping yard sale finds is supposed to be fun!

Tools and Materials

Folded Cone-Shaped Bark Shade

Make sure you have a piece of bark long enough to fold into a cone. The 10" tall, 7" diameter shade pictured here required a sheet of bark 15" by 30". You will also need scissors for cutting the bark to size and two or three large brass paper fasteners, which are widely available at office supply stores. A marking pencil and compass are handy to help mark the curved bottom. A purchased clip-on wire shade adapter attaches the bark shade to the bulb.

METHOD

1. Fold the birchbark sheet into a cone shape. Adjust the size to suit the lamp. Hold the shade steady with one hand while you secure it with brass fasteners through the two pieces of bark.
2. Adjust and slightly mold the shade while the bark is still supple.
3. Arrange the cone over the clip-on wire shade adapter.
4. Using heavy-duty thread and a sharp needle you may choose to stitch the cone shade to the wire adapter in three or four places or simply place the cone over the adapter. It will usually rest there and require no further attachment.

FIG. 19-1

$\mathcal{L}$amps are often among the most intriguing items at yard sales. Tall lamps and short lamps, pottery and plastic lamps, figurine, ginger jar and candlestick lamps, all cover the tables at flea markets and tag sales. Rustic revamping is intended to help you develop your own style and very often the funny little lamps you rescue from oblivion can be given just as much appeal as expensive antiques. Learn to trust your own taste. Remember, it is the jolt of unexpected combinations that sets these lamps apart from the realm of pure function.

About Lamps

$\mathcal{A}$ few simple rules should be observed when buying second-hand lamps or any electrical fixture. If there is an outlet available at the site, ask the seller to plug it in and turn it on to determine whether it works.

Repairing Lamp Fixtures

If the lamp fails to function properly, the difficulty may be in the cord, providing the outlet is in working order. If the switch contacts are so badly worn that the switch will not function, the socket will have to be replaced with a new one. Frayed lamp cords must be replaced, and unless you are skilled at electrical wiring, repairs and replacements are best left to professional electricians. Small electrical repair shops will be listed in the Yellow Pages of your phone book.

The maximum wattage for small table lamps is 60 watts, and for lamps with bark or vine shades it is 40 watts. (Helpful hint: Appliance bulbs, intended for use in stoves and refrigerators, come in 25 and 40 watts, and are the perfect size for small shades.)

20
RoosterLamp

With a Bark Base & Laminated Shade

This three-dollar rooster lamp now helps to warm up winter evenings with the soft light that glows from under its pieced shade. Paper-thin bark strips applied diagonally to the base harmonize with the cottony white color of the rooster and add a natural texture. I used ½" finishing nails to attach the bark, incorporating their silvery nail heads into the pattern of the bark. For pleasing overall symmetry, a laminated bark shade was added.

Tools and Materials

You will need a purchased paper shade; commercial-grade fast-set adhesive; spring-type clothespins (or similar clamps) to hold the pieces together while they are drying; paper and tracing paper for making a pattern; scissors; a utility knife (optional); a pencil and measuring tape.

You will also need an assortment of thin, dry birch-bark pieces. If the bark is not dry it will separate from the glue as it dries. The bark can easily be peeled in thin layers, almost like the skin of an onion. Use both sides of the bark to take advantage of the color variations. (*Note:* If you cannot find natural birchbark sheets, consider using flexible wood veneer, such as oak or ash, sold through woodworking shops and catalogs.)

Making the Laminated Shade

The shade is constructed in eight sections; four trapezoidal pieces are applied first, followed by four overlapping rectangles. These sections may be traced and cut directly on the bark, but for accuracy it is best to make the paper pattern first. (*Note:* The bark is applied to a covered shade, not a wire frame).

1. Place a piece of paper on a flat surface. Lay the shade on the paper, marking the paper along the top and bottom of the shade.
2. Roll the shade over the paper and continue to mark the paper along the top and bottom as you roll.
3. Cut out the paper pattern and, holding it against the covered shade, adjust any inaccuracies in the shape.
4. Fold the pattern in half and then in half again (see Figure 20-2 and 20-3).
5. Cut the four shapes out and trace them onto the back of the birchbark. Cut out the shapes on the bark.

METHOD

FOLD ONCE

FIG. 20-1

FOLD TWICE

FIG. 20-2

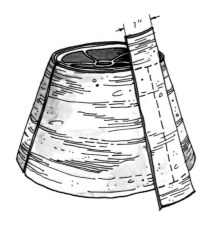

FIG. 20-3

6. When you have all four bark pieces cut to size, spread glue on the back surface of one piece of bark and press into place. Adjust the top and bottom edges for a perfect fit.

7. Using the clothespins, clamp the bark to the shade along the top and bottom rims.

8. Repeat with the remaining three trapezoidal pieces. Allow the glue to dry overnight.

9. To make the overlapping rectangles: Cut 1" wide strips of bark at least as long as the shade is high (Figure 20-3.)

10. Spread glue on the back of one piece. Press in place, making sure of a snug fit. The strips cover the joints of the trapezoidal pieces by at least ½" on either side.

11. Secure with clothespins along the top and bottom rims.

12. Repeat with the remaining three pieces. Allow to dry overnight, and trim any excess with a utility knife, if necessary.

21

Fireplace Lamp

With a Laced Bark Basket Shade

Sometimes I feel like Alice in Wonderland as I encounter all sorts of startling lamps such as this marvelous fireplace lamp that appeared at a Friday evening auction. With its frayed wiring and thick layer of dust and grime, it did not appeal to the majority of the bidders, most of whom were there for the pre-advertised tools. At eight dollars I considered it a great bargain and perfect for my den. Call it kitsch, or call it funky, there is a humorous element to the rustic camp style that this lamp exemplifies. Discovering such a unique item also means rediscovering your own spark of creativity as you envision how to turn it into a usable object again.

After I rewired and thoroughly cleaned the lamp, it was ready for a shade. I don't know what size or shape of shade its creator had intended, but I think my addition of an oval, laced bark shade is perfect.

Tools and Materials

You will need garden shears; a marking pencil and a measuring tape; an awl or leather hole punch; spring-type clothespins for holding parts together while lacing; pliers; sharp scissors; paper to make a pattern; a large-eyed needle and twine, bark strips or raffia for lacing; a wire shade armature; wire cutters; two pliable willow shoots, approximately ¼" in diameter and 46" long; and two pieces of flexible birchbark, each approximately 10" by 22".

Making a Basket Shade

1. Cut two pieces of bark into a trapezoid, with the bottom approximately 3" larger than the top (Figure 21-1).
2. Using the awl or hole punch, punch holes evenly approximately 1" apart along the two sides of both pieces of the peeled bark sheets.
3. Using a back stitch, lace the sides together. (*Note:* You may choose to lace all parts together with the needle and twine for increased strength and then add the peeled bark or raffia for embellishment.)
4. Using the awl or hole punch, make two rows of holes along the top and bottom edges of the bark sheets, approximately 1" apart and 1" away from the edge (Figure 21-2). Trim the top and bottom edges at this

METHOD

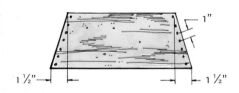

FIG. 21-1

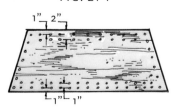

FIG. 21-2

time to even out any irregularities. Keep at least ½" between the edges and the closest row of holes.

5. Carefully bend one pliable willow twig into an oval and fit it carefully outside the top rim. Clamp the twig to the bark with clothespins to hold it in place until the lacing is completed.

6. Join the bark to the oval twig using twine or bark strips, by lacing through the holes diagonally over the branch and through the bark. The twine is simply tied in a double knot and the ends are tucked under the lacing.

7. Repeat steps 5 and 6 with the remaining willow twig along the bottom rim.

8. To add the wire shade support use the wire cutters to remove the spokes and bottom rim from the wire shade armature. Because most lampshades are round, you will have to create an oval shape using pliers or a bench vise, to fit inside the bark shade.

9. Place the shade support inside the bark shade, approximately 2" down from the top rim. Using heavy-duty thread and a sharp needle, stitch the bark shade to the wire shade support in four or five places (Figure 21-3).

FIG. 21-3

22

Jug Lamp

With a Five-Sided Laced Bark Basket Shade

There always seems to be an abundant supply of jug lamps offered at flea markets and tag sales. Women's magazines in the thirties and forties often included simple instructions for recycling jugs and bottles into table lamps with purchased socket/wire kits. Many Depression-era women followed these directions and used various sizes of pottery jugs and straw-bottomed Chianti bottles to fabricate lamps—the same lamps that are now making their way into yard sales.

This two-handled jug is a good example of home-made lamp making, and its narrow neck and rounded shape seemed perfectly suited for the curved five-sided wire frame I had been keeping for something special. Even the plastic ruffles that originally covered the frame didn't frighten me. I knew I would be able to make good use of the shape and reinterpret it in bark. Often the base suggests the shade, but in this case, the shape of the shade came first and I was delighted to find such a suitable base.

Tools and Materials

You will need a measuring tape and marking pencil; an awl or leather hole punch; wire lampshade frame; heavy twine and large-eyed needle; a piece of paper big enough to accommodate the size of your shade. (*Note:* Adjust the size of the pattern as necessary.)

METHOD

Making the Shade Pattern

1. Place a piece of paper on a flat surface. The paper should be as large as the frame's circumference. Lay the frame on the paper, marking the paper outside the top and bottom wires along one spoke.
2. Roll the wire frame over the paper and mark the paper along the top and bottom wires as you roll (Figure 22-1).
3. Allow at least an extra ¼" on all four edges to permit a final trimming. Remember that each section of the frame will have its own pattern piece. Cut out the paper pattern and, holding it against the frame, make any necessary adjustment.
4. Trace pattern pieces on the back of the birchbark. Cut out the sections.
5. Mark holes on the front of the bark, along the top and bottom at ½" intervals. These holes should be about ½" above the bottom and below the top of the shade.

FIG. 22-1

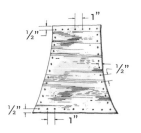

FIG. 22-2

FIG. 22-3

Making the Shade

1. Mark holes on the front of the bark, along the sides, at ½" intervals. Mark the holes along the sides so that when the sections are butted together the connecting holes are ¼" from the edge (Figure 22-2).

2. Using the awl or hole punch, punch out all the holes from the front of the bark, at the marked intervals.

3. Knot the twine at one end so that it will not pass through the hole Figure 22-3). Working from the front, lace the top and bottom bark sections over the wire edge, and draw it through each hole from the front using an overcast stitch.

    Leave enough slack while lacing the top and bottom so that each section can be adjusted once the sides are laced in place.

4. Lace two sides to each other, and over a vertical wire spoke, using an overcast stitch. Continue lacing all the side sections together (Figure 22-4). When the sides are laced, they should lace on a diagonal (Figure 22-5).

5. Once the sides are laced in place, adjust the top and bottom sections if necessary. Check to make sure all sections are tight.

6. Slipstitch the end of the twine to the knot at the beginning, or tie off with a double half knot.

FIG. 22-4

FIG. 22-5

23

Flatiron Lamp

With Grapevine Weaving

My favorite lamps are the homemade originals created out of old objects, like this flatiron lamp. Relieved from active duty, the iron's sturdy form was welded to an 8" length of pipe, and recycled into a whimsical 12" tall lamp base. Painted a tarnished gold, the forlorn little lamp was sitting on the half-price table at a late September tag sale. Priced at a dollar and fifty cents, it beckoned.

Its graceful shape took on new personality when I dabbed a thin coat of flat black acrylic paint over

the gold, giving the whole thing a patina of age. Although the flatiron was originally black, painting it a solid color would have made it look too much like a reproduction. The lightly applied black paint helps to give it a slightly weathered look. To achieve this effect I used a sponge and applied the paint with a light, pecky hand. If you use water-based (latex) paint, make sure your sponge is wrung out and fairly dry. Natural sponges work best. Cellulose sponges leave hard edges in the paint and are not suitable for sponge painting. If you don't have a natural sponge, or prefer to use an oil-based paint, substitute a soft, wadded-up cloth that can be discarded afterwards.

Tools and Materials

For this project you will need a wire lampshade frame; garden shears or clippers for cutting vines; and an ample supply of local vine, such as grapevine, wisteria, moon seed or Virginia creeper. To make your weaving easy, gather the vines in the summer, strip them of their leaves, and weave the green vines. When they dry on the frame, they will be very durable. If you have to use winter vines, soak them in warm water to make them flexible.

This 8" by 6" wire frame with its clip-on top was just the right size and shape for the flatiron lamp. It needed only some simple grapevine weaving to shield the glare of the bulb. Never allow a wire lampshade frame to slip by at a sale. Always be on the lookout for old, used, broken or discarded lampshade forms, or other types of wire forms such as wire baskets and containers. Wire frames work best for vine weaving and for lacing bark, but paper shades can be a good foundation for glued-on bark, or tacked-on vines. It is a good idea to have a ready supply of shades on hand so you will have a choice of shades for your base. If you wind up with more wire shades than you need, you can always weave them with supple vines and turn them into sturdy baskets.

Vine Lampshade

Lampshade frames usually have an even number of spokes, so the usual method of weaving "under and over" is not suitable.

METHOD

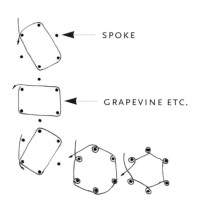

SPOKE

GRAPEVINE ETC.

FIG. 23-1

1. Begin at the top of the shade. Pull the first vine under one metal rib and over two ribs, carefully tucking the exposed ends under the rows of vines as you weave.
2. Continue this pattern for five or six rows.
3. With the end of a length of vine long enough to manage comfortably, pull the vine under one rib and loop it over the same rib. Moving in one direction, pull the vine under the next rib and loop it over that rib. Repeat this pattern until you have completed one row.
4. Begin the next row by pulling the vine under one rib and over two ribs. Push each row of vine weaving up toward the completed weaving as you work, to ensure a tight weave.
5. Begin the next row, weaving under and over the same rib as in step 3.
6. Begin the next row, weaving under two and over one.
7. Repeat steps 4, 5 and 6 until you reach the bottom of the shade.
8. To complete the shade, wrap the vine in a diagonal loop under and over the last two rows of vine, including the wire frame rim.

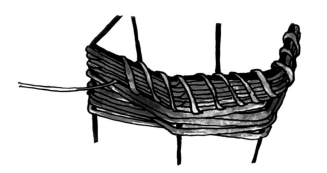

FIG. 23-2

24

Maple Syrup Can Lamp

With an Edged Lamp Shade

When I saw this Vermont maple syrup can for sale at a garage sale for two dollars I grabbed it for a good friend who lives in a city apartment, but who once confided to me that he dreams of owning a little cabin in Vermont. I quickly transformed the can into a lamp using a simple kit I purchased at a hardware store. Virtually anything can be turned into a lamp base, and for the rustic camp look you may want to consider flower pots, fishing or game club trophies, enamel coffee pots, candlesticks or toy sailboats, to name just a few of the possibilities.

I bought this shade (and the lamp that came with it) for eight dollars at a local discount store. I am sure that I will find some use for the lamp later.

METHOD

1. To give the shade the rustic camp look I used colorful Indian beads and hemlock pine cones to trim the bottom of the shade. Using a spool of 24-gauge wire and a package of colorful beads from a craft store, I began by stringing five beads on the wire.
2. I then wound the wire around the top petals of hemlock cones, and strung another five beads.
3. I continued stringing and looping the wire around the hemlock cones to create a garland long enough to go around the circumference of the shade.
4. The garland is attached using a needle and strong thread.

Your options for making lamps are endless. Empty food containers such as large olive oil or tomato juice cans are given a new lease on life when turned into table lamps. Be on the lookout for colorful printed cans (rather than those with a paper label) to help create the perfect accent for your room. You can stack tins on top of one another to make a taller lamp.

Remember, topping off your lamp with just the right shade will make all the difference between tasteful and tacky. Natural linen shades will suit almost every lamp base but you may also want to try your hand a creating a theme lamp. Consider hanging a trim of corks from a shade topping a converted wine bottle or miniature wooden tomatoes (from the doll section at your local craft store) on a shade topping a large juice tin. A coffee tin base and a shade trimmed with tiny dangling spoons and decoupaged with color copies of vintage coffee advertisements would be a fun addition to almost any kitchen or breakfast room. While it is true that lamps are especially appropriate in casual rustic settings, many of today's informal rooms can also benefit from the addition of an utterly fanciful lamp. Tag sale and theme lamps help

brighten up some starkly sophisticated and sparse houses with a small dose of eclectic charm and rustic nonsense.

Some suggestions for making lamp bases include candlesticks, stoneware jugs, canning jars, milk bottles, motor oil cans, watering cans, porch pillars, birdhouses, bird feeders, duck decoys, and discarded children's toys. Toy drums, trucks, and sailboats, or letter blocks spelling out a message or a name would all make charming theme lamps. One of the sweetest lamps I ever came across was a made from a child's well worn cowboy boot. It sat on the desk of the CEO of a large company. It was his child's boot, and he smiled as he told me that his wife had transformed it into a lamp for him as a surprise anniversary gift.

*T*ry to select a shade that is wider than the base of your lamps. This is most important with floor lamps where the shade and the base are far apart and keep in mind that the taller the lamp the greater the width difference ought to be. Lamp necks may show but sockets ought to be hidden. One way to hide a socket is with a dangling garland trim, such as is shown on the Maple Syrup Can Lamp. A fabric ruffle, fringe, or pom pom trim can be also be added to the edge of a shade to hide the socket.

A Note About Shades

Purchased shades with a smooth surface can look great with images decoupaged onto them. Some suggestions for decoupage materials include postal stamps, seed packets, stickers, paper leaves, newspapers, paper labels from cans, wine labels, maps, wallpaper, fabric, greeting cards, and gift wrap paper. Consider making photocopies of family photos, vintage postcards, scrapbook pages, letters, diaries, song sheets, children's drawings and even report cards and decoupaging those onto your shade for a whimsical effect.

Some ideas for shade trims are sea shells, beads, pearls, Christmas tree garlands, buttons, thimbles, jewelry findings, thumb tacks, bottle caps, corks, nutshells, and coins, particularly ones gathered on your travels to different countries.

25
Gilded Twig Lamp

With a Bucket Shade

Two diverse components are joined together to make this elegant handcrafted lamp, which creates an element of surprise and humor. Another few months and this rusted-out bottomless remnant of a bucket would have been completely lost to the elements. I rescued it from its hiding place under some brush and wet leaves nestled along a tumbling stone wall on a path in the Catskill Mountain woods surrounding my house. With the addition of a wire shade rim pressed into position, this one-of-a-kind lampshade is a tribute to the possibilities in recycling.

Tools and Materials

You will need a lamp-making electrical kit (available in most hardware stores); an electric drill with a selection of bits; a hammer; three 1" box nails (or any common flathead nails); a plumb bob; acrylic gold paint (ask at your local craft or art supply store about metallic paints products); three ½" diameter, 21" long twigs for the lamp base; one 3" diameter, 1" thick wood slice for socket support/leg topper.

(*Note:* Old rusty buckets are not very heavy and that is what makes them desirable lampshades. If you were to use a new bucket, however, I would suggest removing the bucket bottom with a hacksaw or tin snips and drilling pairs of holes around the bucket in order to press or lace the wire shade rim securely to the bucket.)

1. To build the lamp, mark the center of the 3" diameter wood slice. Drill a hole wide enough to accommodate the electric socket and thread the wire through.

2. Arrange the three legs along the underside of the wood slice. The twigs are gilded with liquid gold leaf (available at some craft shops and most art supply stores). Acrylic gold paint may also be used. (*Note:* The three legs cross each other at approximately 3" down from the top.) Nail each leg in place through the top of the slice.

3. Drill pilot holes through each leg where they cross. Using thin box nails, attach legs at this location.

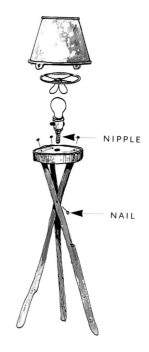

NIPPLE

NAIL

FIG. 25-1

METHOD

FIG. 25-2

4. Stand the lamp upright. Hang a plumb bob from the wood slice to see that the lamp stands straight. Use clippers and a sharp knife to adjust the ends, if necessary.

5. Add electrical components according to the directions on the purchased kit.

26

Wall Sconce

With Wattle Weaving

Rustic wall sconces are simple to make using a half-round wire planter, originally intended to hold flowering plants against a garden wall. This hand-crafted wall light, made in a few hours with flexible twigs and grapevine, has "rustic cabin" written all over it. Its rough texture adds drama to a blank wall. The woven willow and wire sconce is perfect for lighting a narrow hallway, helping to create a mood in a bedroom or adding drama in the dining room.

The multi-colored striped effect is achieved by using a variety of twigs: willow, red dogwood, hazel and pin cherry. Grapevines with their wonderful curlicue tendrils provide added texture and help to fill in the open spaces.

METHOD

1. To make this sconce, weave supple branches and grapevine under and over the existing curved framework of a half-round wire planter (available new at most garden centers).
2. Push each row of weaving up toward the completed weaving as you work, to ensure a tight weave.
3. Trim the ends with garden shears.
4. Install a 25- or 40-watt purchased lamp kit through the back.

Warning: Make sure that the twigs clear the bulb by at least 3".

27

KitchenUtensils

With Twig Handles

When you realize that you do not have to be bound by convention you will find inspiration and ideas by using old things in new ways. It began for me when my favorite old spatula lost its handle, and I replaced it with a twig. The newer, longer twig handle made the spatula easier to use in the kitchen, as well as on the outdoor grill, and its extended branch makes a useful natural hanger. Soon after I saved my spatula, I found a kitchen fork

that was missing its handle in the bottom of my mother's cutlery drawer. I replaced the fork handle with a twig too, much to my mother's delight. Soon I was getting requests for whole sets of flatware and utensils with twig handles.

Tools and Materials

Almost any type of spoon or fork can be cut with a hacksaw. Knives, however, are a different story. Many old one-piece knives have weighted handles, and are difficult to cut. While some one-piece knives, such as butter spreaders and fruit knives, are lighter and can be cut like the forks and spoons, there is often an abundance of cracked and broken plastic-handled knives around at house sales. This type of knife blade is easily separated from its original handle.

Any hardwood, such as beech, birch, cedar or willow, approximately 9" long and ¾" in diameter may be used for the kitchen utensils; and 4" to 5" long and ½" to ¾" in diameter for the flatware. Handles are trimmed to fit after they are installed, so select twigs that are longer than you need. When gathering twigs keep in mind that the handles should feel comfortable in your hand. Try them out before you install them.

You will need a crosscut handsaw (for utensil handles); garden shears; a ruler; a marking pencil; a hammer; sandpaper (optional); a drill with a selection of bits; a vise for holding the twig steady while drilling, and holding the utensil steady for placement. This can be a bench vise or a portable hand vise. You may also need a sanding disk, grinding wheel or hand file to form the tang shape.

Note: Before electric drills there were hand drills, and these are still used today with great success. A serviceable

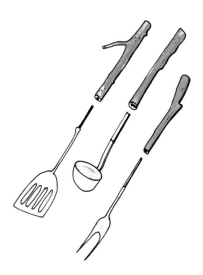

FIG. 27-1

hand drill can accommodate bits ¼" to ⅜" in diameter, which makes them perfect for these small projects. If you are planning on making several five-piece settings, however, you will want to use a power drill to help make the job go quickly. Battery-powered cordless models are also available, but for steady service a moderately priced electric drill is definitely the best option.

Removing Old Handles

Use a hacksaw to remove the old handle. To fit most utensils or flatware into a twig handle, their utensil shaft is altered beforehand. Using a handfile or grinding wheel, shape the utensil ends as pictured (Figures 27-2).

The squared-off ends, known as *tangs*, are fitted into the twig handles.

METHOD

1. Measure and mark the center top of each twig.
2. Using the correct sized drill bit, drill a hole at the center mark of each twig, slightly smaller than the handle. (*Note:* Precautions should be taken when drilling into the center of a twig. NEVER hold the small twig in your hand while drilling, and if you place a round twig in the jaws of a vise to hold it steady, you will probably crush or mar the twig. A simple woodworking solution is to wrap the twig with a soft, dense fabric before placing it in the vise.) You are now going to place a square peg in a round hole.
3. Place the utensil in the jaws of the vise to hold it steady. Place the handle in the hole and firmly tap it into place using a hammer. Trim the ends to size. Use sandpaper for a smooth finish, if desired.

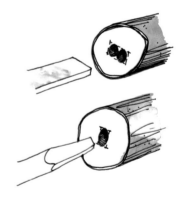

FIG. 27-2

TANGS

28

Garden Utensils

With Twig Handles

Twig handles for garden hand tools seems like such a natural idea that I'm sorry I didn't think of it sooner. Wonderful old trowels and weeders are always appearing at moving sales, and very often the quality of these old tools is superior to modern models. Sometimes all they need to put them back in working order is a good rubbing with steel wool, and a new handle.

Garden hand tools have a metal collar that surrounds the handle. To insert the handle in the collar, whittle the end of the twig to size and attach with screws through the existing holes.

FIG. 28-1

29

Flatware

With Twig Handles

Welcome your guests with your own personal style and learn the art of contemporary table setting by using an imaginative mix of accessories. Homemade rustic flatware combines the natural with the sophisticated to create just such a mix and help individualize a dining table. Used outdoors, they make a friendlier statement than plastic and help to showcase a good recycling technique. Fun to make, comfortable in your hand, heavy and inexpensive—what more can you ask of flatware? Just keep in mind that they should not be placed in the dishwasher. (See Project 27: Rustic Utensil Handles for method.)

30

Glassware

With Twig Bases

Marvelous for entertaining as well as everyday use, branch-stemmed glassware is the ultimate for creating a rustic atmosphere. If you're making these for yourself, consider making a few extra to give as an imaginative gift, along with a bottle of bubbly. White birch is especially attractive for the "stems," but any hardwood may be used. The finished stems are 4" to 5" long and approximately 1¾" in diameter. Old wide-bowl champagne glasses, plentiful on the garage sale circuit, make excellent dessert dishes for ice cream or pudding. If their stems are broken or bases chipped, as they often are, make 2" tall, 2½" diameter branch bases for them.

Note: Be extremely careful when working with glass. Always wear safety goggles and heavy work gloves. If you run out of broken stemware, and want to make new wooden stems, place the glass stem in a paper bag. Holding the glass bowl in one hand, and with the stem inside the bag, use a hammer and a sure, quick stroke to strike the stem. When the stem breaks, the shattered glass remains in the bag, making it easy to dispose of. This takes a little practice, but after a while you will develop a sure touch.

METHOD

1. Using the same technique as for the utensil and flatware handles, mark and drill holes to accommodate the cut stems.
2. Squirt a dab of commercial-grade adhesive in the hole, insert the stem and allow the glue to dry before using.

As with the flatware and the utensils, the glassware is definitely not for the dishwasher.

31

Fireplace Tools

With Twig Handles

I was thrilled to get this heavy set of brass fireplace tools for only five dollars, even though some of the handles were missing. I removed all the rest of the handles and replaced them with twigs, creating a rustic set such as those often found in mountain cabins.

Tools and Materials

You will need a single-bit axe for felling trees; a crosscut hand saw; a ruler or measuring tape; a drill and a selection of bits; a wood screw stud and a connecting nut with machine threads (available at hardware stores) to attach a twig to a tool. Always use safety goggles and work gloves. You will also need a hardwood twig, such as birch, maple, cherry or hickory, ½" to 1" in diameter and 8" to 25" long.

Because fireplace tools come with threaded rods, it is necessary to get the right threaded parts from the hardware store. The stud has a wood screw bottom and a machine thread top; the connecting nut is made up entirely of machine threads. To ensure a proper fit, take a diagram with you to the hardware store.

1. Using a drill bit slightly smaller than the diameter of the stud, drill through the center of a twig handle to accommodate the stud. (*Note:* Soak the twig handle in water for 15 minutes to reduce the chance of it splitting when the stud is inserted.)
2. With a larger bit to accommodate the connecting nut, continue drilling.
3. Connect the stud to the nut.
4. Connect the threaded tool rod to the nut and install the twig. To remove the handles, simply unscrew the handle.

METHOD

FIG. 31-1

32

Twig Ledge

Photo Gallery

Designed for practicality, this natural ledge creates a rustic home gallery for displaying favorite photos and framed art. Various lengths of twigs are secured to the wall with 2" drywall, Phillips head screws and a power drill. If used over a desk in a home office, clippings, bills and memos can be attached to the extended twigs with clips and hooks.

RUSTIC ORIGINALS

Revamping Furniture Finds

Making Twig Furniture & Household Things   Abby Ruoff

MAKING TWIG GARDEN FURNITURE   Abby Ruoff

Weddings with more Love than Money   Abby Ruoff

Making Twig Furniture & Household Things

PART 2

Folk Art
for Rustic Revisions

*W*HAT IS FOLK ART?

"Folk art" is a subject unto itself. Volumes have been written to explain and evaluate its appeal, often with differing opinions. Not everything old, colorful and handmade is folk art, but for the purpose of this book it is the art of the people, who, using available materials, have created the bright utilitarian and decorative objects that most of us have come to think of as folk art. Its present appeal is related to our desire to return to a simpler time; a time when ordinary folks with imagination were revamping with twigs and paint, sometimes out of necessity and other times just for the simple joy of it.

Folk Art Colors

From the bright, primary colors of the Pennsylvania Dutch Hex signs to the soft tints found on Shaker painted furniture, we have inherited a rich palette and been introduced to a wide range of color intensities in folk art pieces. Traditional folk art colors project brightness, clarity and contrast as found in antique quilts, pottery and painted tin. From gentle butter white to vivid tomato red, a wide range of tones is appropriate, but they all have one thing in common: clarity. Rich and diverse, folk art colors are never muddy.

Always begin with clear, fresh colors. Use flat or semigloss water-based paints for folk art projects. If you desire a high-gloss finish, apply coats of medium acrylic gloss (or polyurethane varnish) over the painted finish.

Folk Art Colors

Whether you are out to camouflage a relic, or simply breathe new life into a tired old piece, making do and making new is definitely the sign of the times and paint is often the answer. Try adding purple and orange dots to a hand-painted stand (see Project 34: Folk Art Pedestal); wood grain a box pink and green (see Project 51: Faux Faux Writing Box); you are the folk artist, so have fun and keep it playful. Aside from natural wood twig furnishings, nothing complements the easygoing charm of the rustic camp look better than these objects that welcome the spirit and warm the heart.

A Note About Green

Some accessories lend themselves perfectly to the rustic camp style and, as often as not, these accessories are green. If I had to pick one color that best captures the cozy cabin feeling of the thirties, when family camps and cabins were in their heyday, it would have to be that vintage shade of aqua green. Everything from kitchen gizmos such as flour sifters, wooden-handled cooking utensils and jar openers to various kinds of furniture was produced in this shade of green and many of these items can still be found at flea markets today.

For that no-place-like-home feeling, think jade green Bauer pottery jugs, green Fiesta mixing bowls, and the highly collectible jadite-colored Fire King dishes. Lime-green slipcovers can cool summer chairs, forest green shutters can frame a door, and green rocking chairs and Wellingtons help conjure up thoughts of cabin porches. Whether it is the check on a dish towel or the soft green of some egg cups and enameled tin dishes, green is the nostalgic color of choice for today's rustic camp style.

33

Round Table

Folk Art Painting & Motifs

L et your imagination loose and give a worn little table a whole new look with mix-and-match paint. Here are some simple steps for painting a small piece.

Tools and Materials

You will need 1" and 2" disposable foam brushes; a #3 round brush for painting the pattern; a pattern and tracing paper; a pencil; acrylic paints in wine purple, willow green, royal blue and harvest

gold; satin polyurethane varnish or acrylic gloss medium (optional) if a protective coat is desired.

METHOD

1. Lightly sand the surface using 150-grit sandpaper.
2. Wipe off the dust with a tack cloth, available at hardware stores.
3. Using any folk art color in a flat latex paint, brush on the primer coat.
4. Allow the piece to dry. Apply latex or acrylic paint in the colors of your choice to different parts of your table, as shown on page 113, using the folk art color sample.

FIG. 33-1

34

Pedestal

With Folk Art Colors & Decoupage

This funny little handmade pedestal is typical of the unexpected surprises that await you at yard sales. It was very sturdy and well built, but in dire need of revamping. By adding dynamic colors and decoupaging stickers onto it, this quirky little item was turned into a piece of folk art.

Tools and Materials

You will need acrylic paints in sage green, purple, orange and mustard yellow; 1½" and 2" disposable foam brushes; a pattern and tracing paper; a pencil; purchased stickers; and decoupage medium.

METHOD

1. The entire piece was first painted with two coats of sage green acrylic paint.
2. The trim colors of purple, orange and mustard yellow were added with a sponge brush.
3. Purchased stickers were pressed on firmly in a random pattern and then sealed with six coats of decoupage medium, allowing enough time for each layer to dry. Stickers usually require at least five coats of sealer to ensure a smooth finish. (For specific instructions on decoupage, refer to Project 52: Serving Tray with Decoupage and Twig Handles).

35
Cabinet

With Folk Art Painting & Motifs

Fifty dollars for the cabinet and fifty dollars to have it delivered! I hope this sideboard will give you an idea of what can be achieved with a little confidence, pencil and paint. The elegant lines and narrow proportions of this piece appealed to me when I spotted it at a country auction. Even though it had a chipped, dreary dark brown finish, it was solid and well built. Thankfully I was not intimidated when I overheard someone in the audience whisper, "What

an eyesore," just as the auctioneer shouted out "Sold to Number Seven!" because I was holding Number Seven. I wish they could see it now—transformed with the magic of decorative paint.

Tools and Materials

You will need flat latex house paint in off-white and light harvest gold; acrylic paints in sage green and wine purple; a dab of brownish black or "dirty water" (see Project 3: One Drawer Stand With a Twig Drawer & Antiquing) for a wash; disposable foam brushes; a variety of paintbrushes; drawing pencils; and a pattern and tracing paper. (*Note:* Dressmaker's carbon paper comes in light colors and is useful for transferring onto light painted surfaces. You will also need satin polyurethane varnish, or acrylic gloss medium. (It is necessary to apply a transparent finish, in order to protect the pencil work.)

METHOD Begin with a small project or practice board until you feel confident of your ability to achieve soft, muted colors.

1. Thoroughly clean the piece you will be painting, using soapy water and a brush or cloth.
2. Let it dry and then sand it lightly to remove any rough spots.
3. Using the foam brush, apply the off-white latex base coat to the entire piece. Allow it to dry completely.
4. The gentle, flat look of both the green and the yellow areas is achieved by going over the dry colors with a transparent wash and then dragging off the wash so that the first coat shows through. *Note:* You will want to experiment with various tools and develop your own technique for producing a delicate effect.

   To make a wash: Lighten the base colors (in this case green and yellow) with a bit of latex white and enough water to ensure transparency.

   Apply the wash all over the piece, one area at a time, and using a dry bristle or sponge brush, drag it through the wet

wash. You can also try "brushing off" for an uneven finish, which involves applying an even layer of paint and, before it dries thoroughly, using a dry brush or paper towel to brush off some of the paint with a firm, steady hand, through the semi-wet paint.

5. Using a copy machine, enlarge the pattern provided to fit your project.

6. Using the carbon paper, trace the design from your enlargement directly on the furniture.

FIG. 35-1

7. Go over all of the traced lines with a drawing pencil. Vary your stroke to obtain lighter and darker lines, by increasing pressure or using a variety of different types of pencils. *Note:* The pencil lines remain visible on the finished project.

8. Using a watery solution of green, fill in the leaves.

9. Apply a transparent purple wash over the grapes. To emphasize individual grapes, use a pointed, red sable brush, bearing down as you begin the stroke and lifting up as you complete it, much like the cursive C.

10. To add character and a little natural "aging," apply a weak solution of brownish black paint (or "dirty water"). Use a natural sponge, rag or sponge brush to "wash" the piece with the solution. Concentrate mainly on the edges and keep the middle areas clean. Don't overdo this effect. It should appear naturally aged, not dirty.

   Seal with a transparent finish, such as flat polyurethane varnish or an acrylic gloss medium.

36

Cut-Outs

From Rusted or Aged New Tin

Creating tin silhouettes out of rusted old tin is fun, satisfying and amazingly easy. All you really need is some tin and a good pair of tin snips. Try looking in your town dump or the junkyard for rusted tin pieces. If you can't find old tin, new tin sheets can be purchased at building supply stores and some hardware stores.

Aging New Tin

1. Use coarse-grit aluminum oxide sandpaper to create a moderately rough texture.
2. Paint tin with flat-black exterior latex paint.
3. Using a semi-dry natural sponge, dab on red, brown and yellow in a random pattern.
4. Use a transparent finishing coat, if desired.

This technique gives the appearance of rust, especially on small pieces.

The geese shown here are just one example of a suitable shape for cut-out tinwork. Various birds, fish, animals and other simple figures make excellent subjects for tin silhouettes. Look through old books and magazines for inspiration when designing your own cut-outs. Trace your pattern directly on the tin and, using tin snips like scissors, cut out the shape. It is as simple as that! Aside from being charming wall and tree decorations, tin cut-outs can send a welcoming message when placed on a window ledge.

FIG. 36-1

37

Hanging Box

With Punched Tin

Reminiscent of cabin shutters, this pierced tin design enhances a vintage bin. The clean lines of galvanized tin storage boxes and bins are reappearing in many of today's best-dressed homes and offices. While reproduced versions of old tinwork show up in sophisticated catalogs and stylish home decorating shops, tin bread boxes and kitchen canisters are often overlooked at flea markets and yard sales.

I rescued this wonderful double bin from a junk pile, added a classic

tree punched design, and painted its rusty red and white finish with silver metallic paint, to resemble unfinished tin. Now it helps to organize and file household paperwork. If you stop thinking of bread boxes as only for bread, you will see these bins as versatile units that can be displayed everywhere from an office desk to a bathroom wall.

Tools and Materials

Punching tin is a bit time-consuming, but very easy and well worth the effort. The only tools required for traditional tin punching are a nail, hammer and a hammering board. An awl may be used to inscribe lines and punch the holes, but a nail works just as well. An eight-ounce ball-peen hammer is comfortable, but almost any regular hammer will do. For quick and easy tin punching, and to eliminate sharp edges, I like to use an electric drill. For either the traditional or shortcut method, you will need a scrap piece of wood to use for a hammering board or the tin will dent when it is pierced. A pattern, ruler and pencil are used to create the design. Heavy-duty work gloves and safety glasses are a must.

Note: If your tin box is painted, you can either strip off the old paint or simply paint over the existing finish with any number of today's available metallic paints. A good hardware store or paint shop can supply you with spray-on or brush-on metallic finishes that will resemble raw tin or galvanized metal. Use metal primer for automobiles under these paints to achieve an authentic look.

1. Using a copy machine, enlarge the pattern given or create your own.
2. Place the pattern on the front side of the tin and attach with masking tape or adhesive spray-mount.

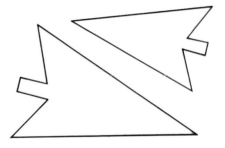

FIG. 37-1

METHOD

3. Using a pencil, trace the pattern on the front side of the tin and remove the paper pattern. Using the pencil and ruler, mark dots approximately 1" apart along the traced lines.

4. For both traditional and shortcut tin punching, place the hammering board on the back of the tin panel and use a hammer and nail to lightly tap the dots, taking care not to actually punch through the tin at this time. This step guarantees a sharp and sure punch.

    Note: By punching from the front, the sharp edges that are formed by the punches remain on the inside and will be less likely to cause injury. Early lanterns and pie safes, however, were often punched from the inside. You may want to practice both methods on a piece of scrap tin before you begin your project. Discarded tin cans are handy for practicing your tin punching technique.

5. Keeping the hammering board in place, traditional punching is achieved by using the hammer and nail to follow the dots and strike the design through the pattern.

    For the shortcut method, use a drill and ⅛" bit to punch the holes.

6. Use one or two coats of auto metal primer to prepare the tin for painting. Finish with metallic aluminum or pewter paint.

38

Tinsel Fish

With Glass Painting

Tinsel pictures, popular during the second half of the 19th century, are American examples of reverse painting on glass. The back side of the glass is painted with translucent colors, much like the 17th-century religious paintings of central and eastern Europe. During the mid-18th century Victorian hobbyists were following the directions given in magazines such as *Peterson's* and *Godey's Ladies Magazine* for painting glass. Crinkled foil was added to give the pictures a distinctive, shimmering effect. The remaining examples of tinsel pictures almost always consist of multi-hued flowers, which were a favorite subject during the Civil War years.

Tinsel art has always fascinated me, and when I wanted something for this pair of tag sale frames, I decided to try a modern version of this folk art, using a fish as a subject. The fins took on a realistic shine with the shimmer of the crinkled foil. Once you learn this simple technique, you will probably want to create your own pictures. Butterflies and beetles with shimmering wings would be another great idea.

Tools and Materials

You will need glass to fit your frame; a black permanent marker; black India ink; inks or dyes for painting glass, available at your local art supply or craft store; aluminum foil; black matte board or oak tag, cut to size; a fish drawing from the pattern provided, an encyclopedia, or other nature book.

METHOD

1. Enlarge fish drawing to desired size on a photocopy machine.
2. Place glass over drawing; trace with a black marker.
3. Add scales, fins, eyes and other details. Accent with colored inks or dyes, leaving some areas unstained.
4. Fill in the outer area with black India ink. Allow all to dry thoroughly. (*Note:* This should only take an hour or two.)
5. Gently crumple a piece of aluminum foil large enough to cover the whole picture. Unfold and smooth the foil so it is evenly wrinkled.
6. Lay the inked side of the glass against the foil.
7. Back the entire work with black matte board or oak tag. Frame as desired.

FIG. 38-1

39

Checkerboard

With Painting & Rustic Checkers

Inspired by memories of yes-teryear, this rustic painted twig checkerboard has check-ers cut from cherry and white birch branches. The board is the perfect topper for the tired old green stand that had been hang-ing around my workroom, but it could be used at the kitchen table just as easily.

Tools and Materials

You will need a pencil and ruler; ½" stencil brush; 1½" sponge

paint brush; 1" finishing nails; a handsaw; a miter box; a drill; and painter's tape. (*Note:* Masking tape may be used but it can pull off some of the paint when removed. Painter's tape is made especially to avoid this problem.) To make the checkerboard you will need a 17" square, ½" to ¾" thick, wood board; four 19" by ½" diameter straight branches for edges; one 12" white birch branch and another with dark bark, each ¾" to 1" in diameter, for the checkers. You will also need dry brush stencil paint in green and yellow; acrylic paint in cinnamon; water-based satin finish varnish; and maple wood stain.

METHOD

To Make the Board

1. With a ruler and pencil, mark a 12" square centered on the 17" square of wood.
2. Draw parallel lines 1½" apart in the 12" square horizontally and vertically, making a grid of 64 squares.
3. Mask out the outer edge of the grid and every other square with tape.
4. Stencil exposed squares green. Let them dry.
5. Remove the tape and tape the painted squares.
6. Stencil exposed squares yellow. Let them dry.
7. Remove tape from the border and tape the inner edge.
8. Paint the border, edges and bottom of the board cinnamon with a sponge brush. Allow to dry.
9. When the entire board is dry, apply a satin finish varnish.

To Make the Edges

1. Cut the 19" branches to fit around the board with 45-degree mitered corners.
2. Pre-drill holes and nail in place.

To Make Checkers

1. Cut twelve ½" to ¾" thick checkers from each lighter (such as birch) and darker branch.
2. Stain the tops of the darker checkers with maple wood stain.

40

Mosaic Frame

With Broken China

The beauty of this folk art mosaic technique is found in the bits and pieces of broken crockery that coat the surface with color and texture. Long before the Watts Towers—the Los Angeles monument of broken china, sea shells and glass fragments—was built, French peasants found delight in decorating items with bits of broken china, a method sometimes called *pique assiette* or mosaic. Around the turn of the century many country folk recycled glistening bits of

patterned china, coins and costume jewelry by embedding them into the sides of jugs and vessels. These "memory jugs" are now high-priced collectibles and are seldom found at garage sales. If you do find one at a reasonable price, be sure to grab it as it will add character to any room.

Tools and Materials

To make your own instant memory frame you will need a selection of chipped and broken china. A caulk gun and container of all-purpose white household caulking (available at hardware stores and building supply shops) are the only other materials required to embellish a picture frame with colorful bits and fragments.

METHOD

1. Work on a hard surface, preferably outdoors. Place the dishes to be broken in a heavy brown paper bag. Place the dishes in the bag on a newspaper and hit them with a hammer. (*Note: Wear safety glasses when breaking china*). Leave the very tiny shards in the bag and discard them. The ideal sized fragment is 1".)
2. Working on one section at a time, coat a wide picture frame with a ½" to ¾" thick layer of caulking.
3. Press the shards into the frame paying attention to size, shape and color. Add more caulk adhesive as needed.

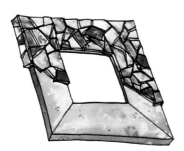

FIG. 40-1

41

Magazine Rack

With Fern Stenciling

The only thing this plain little magazine rack had to recommend it was that it was clean and stained rather than painted, so it was just what I needed to try my hand at fern stenciling. Fern stenciling is an easy, natural decorating technique. I can think of few paint finishes that express the rustic character better than fern printing. Try fern stencils on picture frames, lampshades, boxes, or better yet, doors.

As with any new technique, it is a good idea to try fern printing out first on a scrap of wood. Experiment with the fern placement to achieve different effects. The random pattern shown here can be adapted to a variety of items. For doors, lampshades or picture frames you may want to use ferns of the same size to create a border. Mother Nature is an excellent source for natural stencils, and wonderful patterns can be created using a variety of pressed leaves, grasses and seaweeds.

Tools and Materials

You will need stencil adhesive spray and a can of quick-drying black spray paint. You will also need a variety of fern types if possible. To get a good print they will need to be pressed and dried. (*Note:* To press and dry ferns, gather them in the mid-morning, when the dew has settled but before the noon sun is out. Lay the ferns between layers of clean white tissue paper (or newspaper) and place them on a flat surface in a dry location. Press them with a heavy stack of books or bricks. Ferns usually take seven to ten days to dry.)

METHOD

1. Before you begin, arrange and rearrange the ferns, spore side up, on the surface of the item to be stenciled, until you are satisfied with your composition.
2. Once you are satisfied, spray the front of the fern with a light mist of adhesive and allow it to dry until it is just slightly tacky.
3. Carefully press your ferns into place. Be sure that all the edges are flat in order to achieve a sharp outline when you remove the fern.
4. When all the elements are in place, spray the entire piece you are painting with a light mist of paint.
5. Allow it to dry thoroughly.
6. When it is dry, carefully remove the fern fronds from the object using their stem ends. Remove any small bits of fern sticking to the piece with a commercial adhesive remover or vegetable oil.

42

Hanging Plate Rack

With Painting & Stenciling

Plate racks are hard to find and I considered myself fortunate when this one showed up at our town's annual library/ rummage sale. A plate rack with missing crossbars does appear useless, but if you are thinking twig, it becomes obvious how to put it back into serviceable order. The marvelous flecks of gray/green that marked the sturdy red dogwood branches set the tone for the coloring, and the rack was painted to match.

Tools and Materials

You will need manicure scissors or a utility knife; spray-mount artist's adhesive or stencil spray mount; masking tape; a round stencil brush or bob (see Figure 42-1); and a firm surface on which to cut out your stencil.

Cutting out stencils is a lot easier than you might think. You don't need heavily waxed special paper or architect's linen to cut a stencil any more than a special round brush is required to apply the paint. You can draw your own pattern or use carbon paper to trace your design on any stiff paper, such as a manila file folder. When tracing a pattern, however, a piece of clear, stiff plastic works best. Deli container lids or plastic milk jugs are perfect for creating stencils and an excellent way to recycle the myriad of plastic containers most of us have in our cupboards.

Borrowing from fall foliage, simple oak leaf and acorn stencils are colored with amber and red stencil creams. Stencil creams are solid, concentrated colors, much like shoe polish. They are easy to work with and will not drip. Unlike acrylic paints, these creams dry slowly and the colors may be blended directly on the stenciling surface. They are available at most craft shops and art supply stores.

FIG. 42-1

Making a Stencil

METHOD

1. Enlarge the pattern you want to stencil on a photocopier.
2. Place the clear stencil material, such as a plastic lid, over the pattern, and using a permanent marker, trace the design on the plastic.
3. Use a sharp manicure knife or utility knife to cut out the pattern.

If you are using a utility knife, lay the stencil sheet on a scrap piece of glass or heavy cardboard, and attach it with masking tape to keep it flat. The glass or cardboard prevents the knife from scratching your work surface.

Hold the knife so it is almost perpendicular and apply downward pressure to make a clean cut. Rough edges can be trimmed with manicure scissors.

Stenciling

1. Use artist's spray-mount adhesive or stencil spray mount to position the stencil. (*Note:* Do not use masking tape to position the stencil as it can pull paint off the surface of the object when it is removed.)
2. Lightly spray the back of the stencil; position and press onto the surface.
3. Pour a small amount of paint onto a plastic or glass plate.
4. Using a stencil brush or bob, dip the tip in the paint color. Blot almost all of the paint off before you "pounce" the color inside the cutout area.

While a round stencil brush is often used, it is not required. To achieve a soft muted look, early stencillers applied the paint with a velvet-wrapped finger, or they made "bobs" with cotton and fabric-wrapped sticks, as shown in Figure 42-1.

Hold the brush or bob in an upright position and, with a quick and steady motion, pounce repeatedly inside the cutout stencil. For a shaded look, apply the color heavily around the edges and more sparsely toward the center. (*Note:* If you choose to use paint, use artist's acrylic colors and don't thin the paint because if it is watery it will bleed under the stencil.)

PART 3

Rustic Style faux Finishes

CREATING FAUX FINISHES *that* SUIT THE RUSTIC CAMP STYLE

The dictionary definition of the French word *faux*, meaning "imitation, ersatz, false" neglects to mention the most important element of faux finishes—fun! Faux finishing is all the rage today. Finely grained, expensive woods, as well as marble and stone are the natural materials most often imitated in faux finishes. Itinerant painters as early as the 18th century traveled throughout the New England countryside transforming lowly pine pieces into much-sought-after hardwood lookalikes. While the work of some of these early grain painters was very sophisticated, the majority of the surviving examples is the work of less technically skilled artists. These are the pieces that exhibit the playful style of folk art and the pieces whose style best suits the rustic camp look. So hop on the modern faux finishing bandwagon, but rather than attempting to create a realistic imitation of stone and hardwoods, allow your imagination to run free.

Water-based paints make quick work of false graining, and the results are surprisingly expert. Today's variety of satin colors makes it easy to achieve a soft, flat finish and their quick drying time and easy clean-up make fast work of a project. Use latex house paint and semi-gloss acrylic enamel from the hardware store for large projects, and artist's acrylic for smaller pieces. If you plan to finish many pieces, it is a good idea to purchase the base coat in a large quantity and divide it among smaller containers with tight-fitting lids. I usually have a gallon of custom-colored red brick on hand, for I find this a pleasing base coat for a variety of objects. In choosing colors to suit the rustic camp look, take your inspiration from the great outdoors. Try the green of the aspen, willow or hemlock; the brown of the oak leaf, the acorn and the pine cone; or the red of autumn sugar maples and barns that dot the country landscape. Experiment with a variety of analogous colors and hues. Remember, this is your folk art and you are the artist.

This approach to faux finishing is mistake-proof. If you aren't satisfied with the results of your first try, simply wait an hour or so for the paint to dry and begin again. Try not to overwork your piece. One stroke or dab usually does it. The following techniques can easily be adapted to a variety of large, flat surfaces, such as table tops and doors. While these painted projects do not require a sealer, and are easy to retouch if they remain unsealed, you may choose to add a protective coat to protect your piece from spills. If you use a polyurethane varnish, try to obtain the non-yellowing variety. You will want your top coat to be unobtrusive, adding only a soft sheen. Satin tung oil or furniture polish may be used with excellent results. The quickest and best top coat, however, is an acrylic brush-on or spray finish that will not yellow the surface.

43

Table

With Marbling

When I found this one-drawer stand at a yard sale, I especially liked its nicely shaped splashboard and bottom shelf. The table was obviously sturdy and well made, but I think people shied away from it because it was painted brown. I overheard a young couple discussing how long it would take them to strip it down. I looked at the thick brown paint as a blank canvas, ready for some sort of faux work. Any number of finishes and colors would have been appropriate here, but this one said marbling to me.

Marbling was originally a technique perfected by skilled craftspeople who used it to simulate marble for those who could not afford the real thing. Later, less skilled folk art painters took liberties with the basics of marbling and made it rougher and less realistic than the true-to-life copies that went before. Marbling was done on items that would have been made of marble, such as table tops. Today marbling has become quite fanciful and is used on many objects that would never have been made of stone. It is also done in colors that bear no resemblance to the hues of true marble.

To get ready to marble your piece, look at pictures of real marble and study examples of faux marble in books and magazines. Try to collect samples. The more marble you look at the easier it will be for you to create a marbled look. Faux marble appears on many commercial products today, such as tissue boxes and gift wrap. Do not get discouraged by the apparent complexity of marble. Marbling usually requires more practice than the other faux finishes, but despite the various steps it is easy to learn and goes quickly.

Helpful Hints and Tips

It is important to know that natural marble veins are formed diagonally from top to bottom; they never appear midstream. Although the veins in marble join at some point, they travel in the same direction. It is this seemingly random placement of veins that is the secret of good faux marble.

Several kinds of paint will work for marbling, so experiment with paints you already have on hand. I like to keep the dirty water that collects from rinsed brushes in a covered jar on the workbench. This watery solution of red and black produces a perfect aged brown color wash to add an instant distressed look.

Tools and Materials

You will need a sponge brush; a fan brush; at least one feather, such as a sea gull or turkey feather or one of the long ones available in packages at craft and hobby stores; paper towels or clean rags; a dish of water; a flat-bottomed paint pan or tray; a natural sponge (optional); sandpaper and tack cloth, available from a hardware store, if needed; a pointed #4 red sable brush (optional); brick red latex house paint; black semi-gloss enamel; off-white (or ivory) and red artist's acrylic colors; and non-yellowing acrylic top-coat (optional).

METHOD

Some light sanding may be necessary to prepare the piece you want to marble. Sanding cuts down the shine on old varnish, giving a better foundation for the new paint to adhere to. Use a tack cloth (which can be purchased at a hardware store) to remove any residue after sanding.

1. Working on one section at a time, apply the base color (brick red in this case) to the surface. It is not necessary to allow the paint to dry completely at this point.
2. Using the fan brush, or the edge of a feather, apply the black paint, thinned slightly with water, in several sections. (See Figure 43-1). The semi-wet base coat will mix with the black sections to create subtle hue variations.

FIG. 43-1

Adding the Veins

Two techniques produce veins, and both of them involve feathering.

Method 1

1. Using the off-white or ivory paint, draw in the veins with a pointed red sable brush. While the paint is still wet, spread the veining with a dry fan brush; then pull the feather through the wet paint diagonally across the surface. (See Figure 43-2).
2. Using a natural sponge or feather, soften the edges of the veins with a sure and constant motion. The damp sponge will also blend the colors and lift off any excess paint.

Method 2

1. Dip the feather in the paint, wiping off the excess. With quick, firm movements, draw in the veins with a feather. Use the feather as a brush, being careful to wipe the edges dry between each line. Experiment with wet and dry feathers. Try cutting out some of the spines to add variety to your veining.
2. Press some of the veining with the sponge to soften the edges, but leave some sharp, clean lines as well.
3. Pull the feather lightly across some of the veins sideways to open them up. Vary your method from piece to piece and develop a style of your own.
4. When the veining is complete, use a dry sponge (or the tips of a dry fan brush) and some fairly thick paint to dab on a few random dots of red and white. This helps to introduce irregular texture and add a natural appearance to your work.

Of all the faux finishes, marble is not only the most fun, but more importantly, it allows you to get creative and develop a style that is truly all your own. So gather some marvelous colors, grab a feather from the forest floor or the seashore and go to work.

FIG. 43-2

FIG. 43-3

44

Box

With Putty Graining

You can never have enough boxes to store and hold the myriad objects that accumulate in most households, such as sewing items, kitchen gadgets, office supplies, napkins, candles, stationery, correspondence, bills, and of course, tools. With only one other bidder in the audience at a country auction, my ten-dollar bid won this 10" by 22" wooden box. When I got the box home I decided to try putty graining. Putty graining was also known as vinegar painting, because originally

ground pigment and vinegar were mixed with sugar to create a paint that was slightly sticky and stayed put when patterned with putty. A base coat and a top coat of latex or acrylic paint are required to create a negative print.

Tools and Materials

You will need disposable sponge brushes in various sizes; non-hardening modeling clay (or putty for the traditionalist); and semi-gloss black paint or acrylic artist's paint.

Experiment with a variety of patterning tools, including crumpled paper, plastic wrap, a cork, a sponge or even finger-prints. Early painters often used a chamois bob (made by wrapping soft cotton around a stick and covering it with a piece of chamois cloth so it looks like a ball on a stick or a lollipop) or rolled rags to achieve interesting patterns. Let your imagination run free, just as the itinerant painters who began putty graining did. Light paint is usually applied first, then dark. The pattern is revealed by the partial removal of the top coat of paint. There is nothing to stop you, however, from experimenting with light color over dark. Practice first, experiment with various effects and keep it simple. Knowing when to stop will keep your piece from looking overworked.

METHOD

Begin by cleaning the piece to be painted and sanding any rough areas. This box simply needed to be wiped with a damp cloth. Because it was in such good condition and I wanted to maintain a hint of the original color, I did not use a base coat.

1. Water down the black paint (or other color of your choice) until it is quite thin and then apply it one section at a time.
2. While the top coat is still wet, press in the design with a wadded-up piece of clay (or the patterning tool of your choice), lifting out the top color and leaving space between the shapes. For a more subtle effect, use a light hand.

45

Cabinet

With Combing & Sponging

An example of recycling at its finest, this abandoned mahogany TV cabinet was rescued from the dump! My own version of the classic country combed finish was simple to apply once I cleaned up the old cabinet. I removed the surface dirt with a solution of two parts water to one part bleach. I allowed the whole piece to dry and sanded it lightly to add a slight roughness to the previously glossy surface.

Sponging can be used on walls and floors as well as on furnishings. Combing is another example of a negative process and, as its name implies, it involves pulling a comb-like tool through a wet top coat of paint to reveal the color underneath. For large areas, apply the top coat to one section at a time.

Tools and Materials

You will need flat latex house paint in white, yellow ochre and brick red; acrylic paint in bayberry green; polyurethane varnish; 1" and 2" flat paintbrushes, bristle or disposable sponge brushes, and a 10" flat artist's brush for applying the trim color; a coarse-textured natural sponge for dappling; and combing tool(s).

Combing tools can be purchased at craft stores, but it is easy to make your own. The size of the teeth determines the scale of the design. Everything from cardboard to tree bark to plastic lids may be used. Corrugated cardboard with one side of the cardboard peeled back makes a simple comb with evenly spaced teeth. Stiff paper plates with notches cut with scissors or a single-edge razor blade make handy tools, especially for curved surfaces. If you are using a paper comb it is a good idea to make several before you begin as they will need frequent replacing. I usually make my combs out of window-washing squeegees. I use a utility knife to cut L-shaped notches at irregularly spaced intervals along the stiff rubber edge. The long handle helps me to create the wiggles and wavy lines with a quick and easy motion. Experiment with the spacing and width of the teeth to create different effects.

Use only natural marine sponges for sponging because cellulose sponges will leave hard edges. A clean, flat container (a paper plate or disposable aluminum pan) makes a handy to use as a palette for sponge dipping. Rinse out the sponge from time to time while you are working if it becomes loaded with thick paint.

METHOD

1. Paint the entire piece the base color, in this case yellow ochre.
2. Using a wet rag and your finger, wipe off the still wet yellow paint surrounding the contrasting sections of the piece you are painting.
3. Allow the paint to dry completely.

Sponging

1. Pour a small amount of white paint into a flat-bottomed paint pan. Add a small amount of water until the paint is the consistency of heavy cream.
2. Rinse the sponge in water and wring it out until it is almost dry.
3. Carefully dip the damp sponge onto the surface of the paint in the pan. Do not overload the sponge.
4. Dapple the surface of the cabinet with a light pecky motion to produce a soft look. For a more delicate effect, try a dry sponge and thicker paint. Dappled areas should not be too close together.
5. Work in a random pattern, turning the sponge as you go to avoid a repeat pattern. If you make a mistake, simply paint over it with the base color, wait for it to dry, and begin again.
6. Allow the sponge painting to dry thoroughly before combing.

Combing

1. Apply an even top coat of acrylic green paint within one of the sectioned-off panels to be combed.
2. Working quickly, wiggle and scratch the comb through the wet top coat. (*Note:* I put heavy pressure on the comb at this point to allow some of the original mahogany finish to show through.)
3. Repeat with the remaining sectioned-off panels.

Adding the Trim Color

1. After the sponging and combing layers are dry, paint all edges brick red.
2. Apply a coat of polyurethane varnish to protect the finish.

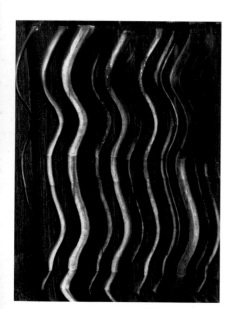

FIG. 45-1

46

Holder

*With Eraser &
Feather Painting*

When I first bought this knitting needle holder from a store display I had no idea what I would use it for, but with its little sectioned-off bins I had faith that it would come in useful someday. When we moved to a new house with a large kitchen island, my knitting needle holder found a home on the island as a receptacle for a growing collection of wooden spoons, rolling pins and assorted kitchen utensils. Throughout the years it has served me well, storing a variety of items throughout

the house. Presently it lives in my workshop and its compartments help to organize paintbrushes, hammers, screwdrivers, rulers, and some of the flotsam and jetsam that makes its way to my workbench.

Tools and Materials

You will need 1" and 2" disposable sponge brushes; Pink Pearl erasers or potato halves; a feather; paper towels or clean rags; non-yellowing acrylic top coat (optional); brick red latex paint; and black semi-gloss enamel.

Cut the erasers into various shapes, such as triangles and ovals, to achieve different looks. Potato halves can be cut into different shapes and used in place of erasers.

Wipe the feather dry between applications. Use a painted board or cardboard to practice feather painting before you begin your project.

METHOD

1. Eraser painting follows the same method as putty graining (see Project 44: Box With Putty Graining). In this example, however, a base coat of black was applied first and allowed to dry, followed by a watery top coat of brick red. Apply the top coat on one side at a time. Lay the piece down flat on its side, or the watery paint will run.
2. Drag your feather through the wet paint with a firm and steady movement.
3. Working quickly while the paint is still wet, press pieces of eraser into the paint along the arched feather line, and the eraser shape will be revealed by the partial removal of the top coat.

FIG. 46-1

47
Coffee Table

With Faux Leather Finish, Staining & Gilding

I considered finding this table without legs a stroke of good fortune. A friend and I had happened upon it at a backwoods yard sale out in the middle of nowhere after we made a wrong turn looking for a place to have lunch. I had been looking for a coffee table for years and felt sure that four old legs were bound to turn up at another sale to support my new table top. Time went by and my hoped-for legs never did appear, probably because some other revamper

was turning them into lamps or candlesticks. I finally cut four 4 by 4's into 10" lengths and attached them to the underside of the table top.

Faux leather painted pieces, while not as common as imitation wood grain or marble, were also favored by those wishing to own a piece of fashionable furniture. Leather-topped tables and desks, some with dyed-leather inlays, were all the rage during the English Regency Period (1793–1820). A swish of orange-brown paint brushed over an ochre base will create the delicate effect of a painted leather-top table. Experiment and have fun with faux leather painting. Try painting plank chair seats red leather, or cigar boxes brown leather.

Tools and Materials

To obtain the delicate effect and subtle texture found in painted faux leather you will need more than one brush, as well as bits of dry, natural sponge and soft rags. A stencil brush and fan brush are used to dab on the flat acrylic colors that help to create the look. An angle brush would be useful to fill in the diamond areas, but any small flat brush or sponge brush will work. Inexpensive, disposable sponge brushes are perfect for painting with acrylic paints and mediums. You will also need painter's tape to mask edges. (*Note:* Masking tape may be substituted for painter's tape, which is available at hardware and paint supply stores, but masking tape will often pull off paint when it is removed.)

A marking pencil and ruler are required for sectioning off the diamond trim; paper towels, soft rags and disposable sponges are needed for staining. You will also require acrylic paint in burnt sienna, burnt umber, yellow ochre, black, and two shades of green—olive and emerald; polyurethane gel wipe-on stain in clear and natural oak; acrylic gold paint and a liquid gold marker (available at craft stores); and lint-free rags and steel wool (optional, but handy for wiping off excess gold).

METHOD

Faux Leather Painting

1. Make sure the wood is clean and sanded before you begin. Apply one or two thin coats of yellow ochre before adding painted shading for the leather look. (*Note:* Look through antique books for examples of leather-top tables to educate yourself and gather ideas and inspiration.)

2. Using a stiff stencil brush, with a light pouncing motion, apply random spatters of burnt umber and sienna sparingly, to one area at a time.

3. To achieve the subtle, natural appearance of leather, dilute the umber with water and take up some paint with the fan brush. Using a quick, steady hand and a jabbing motion, press the bristles down on the surface, creating thin lines, like a chicken scratching.

4. Scatter a few diluted burnt sienna and yellow ochre freckles by spattering spots of paint along the outside edge of the table top, where deeper shading would naturally occur. Let paint dry.

5. Mark off a 1" border around the perimeter of the table, and outline with painter's tape. Using a small artist's brush and black acrylic paint, paint in the black trim.

6. Add yellow ochre trim color.

7. Using the marking pencil and ruler, divide and mark off 2" diamond shapes around the apron. Blend equal proportions of emerald and olive green together and paint the diamonds.

8. The legs are treated to a fanciful graining treatment by combining the colors and techniques used on the table top. Using a dry fan brush, apply a thin layer of burnt umber and burnt sienna to the corners of the legs.

9. Apply a watery, thin wash of green over the umber and sienna, and using a clean rag or paper towel, rub some of the green off before it dries. Brush on a thin layer of yellow ochre and wipe off any excess.

Staining

The variety of stains available today makes it easy to achieve any look you want. Today's stains come in different consistencies and a wide variety of colors, from thin watery liquids that are brushed on, to thicker pastes that are wiped on.

The paste stains both color and protect the surfaces they coat in one easy step. These paste stains are polyurethane resins, with the consistency of petroleum jelly. A textured look can be created using these stains by pressing into them while they are still wet with a rolled rag or even a paper towel. These wipe-on stains are made to be used on new or bare wood, but I have used them successfully on top of previously stained wood as well as on freshly painted surfaces which had been lightly sanded. These paste stains are available in a variety of colors and can be blended to create custom shades.

1. The natural oak gel stain is rubbed over the painted table top. Using a sponge brush or lint-free cloth, apply the stain liberally to the table top in a circular motion.
2. Allow the stain to set for one minute, then wipe off the excess with a clean, soft cloth to achieve a semi-transparent look.
3. Apply the stain over the painted trim and legs in the same manner as the top.
4. Apply additional coats of stain to the top for a darker color. For best results, allow additional coats to dry overnight.

Gilding

Gilding is an overlay technique in which a thin covering of gold, real or artificial, is applied to the surface of an object. True gold leaf is complicated and expensive and not likely to be used by the average revamper on a yard sale treasure. There are, however, many wonderful new and easy methods to gild your work. Available materials for faux gilt include: gold paint in the acrylic or spray-on variety (available at art supply stores, craft shops and hardware stores), liquid gold leaf (available at art supply stores

and some craft shops), imitation gold leaf sheets (available at art supply stores and craft shops), and simplest of all, liquid gold markers (available at art supply stores, craft shops and stationery supply stores). If you aren't afraid to experiment and use a bit of imagination, all these products will work very nicely.

To apply gold paint, liquid gold leaf and gold markers, follow the manufacturer's instructions. (To apply imitation gold-leaf sheets, see Project 48: Roosters With Gold Leaf & Painted Verdigris). To age gilded work, simply apply a wash of acrylic burnt umber or a "dirty water wash" (see Project 3: One-Drawer Stand With Twig Drawer & Antiquing). When the gold is dry, thin the burnt umber paint using a three-to-one ratio. Cover the gold with the wash and, working quickly, dab off the umber with a damp natural sponge.

1. Using the liquid gold marker, outline the green diamonds.
2. Brush the acrylic gold paint on the edges of the legs, removing some paint with your fingers or a dry brush (or steel wool) so the color is uneven.
3. When the gold paint has dried, apply gold marker over the gold paint, again removing some marker on points where the gold would naturally wear off. Continue to add and remove gold until the desired finish is achieved.
4. To preserve your piece, brush or rub on a coat of clear, polyurethane gel wipe-on stain.

48

Roosters

With Gold-Leaf & Painted Verdigris

Chickens like these appear on many a yard sale table. This pair helps to add a touch of sparkle and wit to a rustic cabin. Their garish colors have been coated with thin sheets of gold leaf. Dressing up a cabin with something as unlikely as golden chickens fits the slightly campy style that defines the rustic camp look. The simulated verdigris finish suggests a feeling of antiquity, perfect for some tongue-in-cheek woodland enchantment.

Tools and Materials

You will need a paintbrush; white glue; a pair of porcelain (ceramic) chicken statues; imitation gold leaf sheets (available at art supply stores); blue-green water-based paint.

Gold leaf sheets are as thin as tissue paper and wrinkle at the slightest touch, thus adding texture to your work. To avoid ending up with a patchwork look, carefully tear the sheets into irregular pieces. Overlapping these pieces will give a uniform appearance to the surface. Seal the final layer of gold leaf thoroughly with several coats of the glue to keep the leaf from flaking off.

The corrosion that comes from the natural weathering process of metallic objects leaves subtle hints of color, so try not to overdo the verdigris layer.

Gold Leaf

1. Thin the white glue with a few drops of water.
2. Working on a section at a time, brush the glue on the statue.
3. Press a torn piece of gold leaf onto the glued surface.
4. Apply another coat of glue on the gold leaf.
5. Continue gluing leaf until the surface of the statue is covered, with the edges overlapping. Allow to dry thoroughly.

Verdigris

1. Apply the blue-green paint to small sections of the surface with a dabbing motion.
2. Wipe most of the color away from the wet paint, allowing it to remain in some of the recessed areas.
3. Let dry, and gently brush off any loose leaf.
4. Apply a coat of thinned glue for the sealer coat.

METHOD

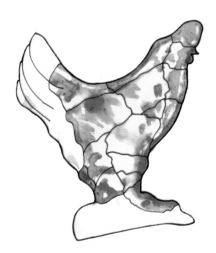

FIG. 48-1

49

Lamp Base

With Marbling, Verdigris & Copperizing

Finding this classic obelisk-shaped lamp in a pile of junk at a flea market is the sort of reward that makes flea markets fun and exciting. Enhanced with layers of different faux finishes, its ordinary metal surface is now extraordinary. Some of the best faux finishes are the result of a poor beginning. This lamp was a perfect example of how there are no mistakes, only happy accidents.

The shape of this lamp seemed perfect for marbling, a technique I was trying to master at the time. As often happens to amateur marblers, I ended up with far too many "veins." Rather than strip it down and start over, I decided to soften the veins with a wash of acrylic copper paint. The marble began to take on a more subtle look under the copper, but still needed some reworking to give it the natural appearance of aged copper. I applied a blue-green wash with a damp natural sponge and while it was still wet, I removed some of it with a lint-free cloth. Finally I ended up with the aged quality I wanted.

Tools and Materials

For marbling, you will need black and white acrylic paint; 1" sponge brush; ¾" long pointed brush; 1 large goose, gull or turkey feather (or a feather from a craft store).

For copperizing, you will require a ½" sponge brush, and/or a natural fan brush and acrylic copper paint, available at art supply and craft stores.

Finally, for verdigris, you will need a natural sponge and blue-green acrylic paint. A matte finish acrylic coat is optional.

METHOD

1. Paint the lamp base with black acrylic paint, using a sponge brush. Allow the paint to dry thoroughly.
2. Paint with a second coat of black paint. Using the ¾" long pointed brush, paint some white veins on the still-wet second coat of paint. (For more thorough marbling instructions, see Project 43: Table With Marbling.)
3. Mix 3 parts white paint with 1 part black paint to produce gray. Draw gray veins across the white veins with the feather, using the feather like a brush. Wipe the edges of the feather dry between each line.

4. After the marble coat is dry, coat a few sections of the base or whatever you are painting with acrylic copper paint. Use a sponge to create a smooth finish.

5. When the copper coat is dry, dab on the blue-green wash with a soft brush, allowing some to drip haphazardly and some random areas of the copper to show through. Additional coats of blue-green paint may be applied to some areas to achieve a natural verdigris finish. (*Note:* A few strokes or dabs usually does it.) There are no mistakes in creating a metallic finish. Each piece is an original.

50

Knife Box

With Rosewood & False Graining

This was not a particularly old or valuable knife box, but its size was certainly impressive so I happily paid eleven dollars for it at a house auction. Every house or cabin needs a few of these versatile painted boxes and they will give you the opportunity to practice grain-painting on a flat surface. Rosewood is one of the easiest woods to counterfeit; I quickly transformed this simple box into a hardwood treasure.

Tools and Materials

You will need barn red flat latex paint; semi-gloss black latex enamel (*Note:* Acrylic paint may be substituted. Both acrylic and latex water-based paints dry quickly and are easy to clean up, and they adhere to wood and metal just as easily as to paper); a 1" or 2" flat paintbrush to apply the base coat; one or two feathers; and a clear acrylic sealer (optional).

METHOD

1. Cover the object with one or two coats of flat red paint, allowing each coat to dry between applications.
2. When the red is dry, combine black paint with water in a container (1 part paint to 3 parts water), mix well and apply the thinned black paint over the red on one side of the piece.
3. Drag the feather in a wavy motion through the still-wet black paint, exposing the red beneath. For different effects, experiment with a comb, feather or wadded-up paper toweling when wiping the top coat away.
4. Repeat step 3 with the remaining sides until the piece is finished.
5. Though not essential, a clear acrylic sealer will help to preserve the finish.

51

Writing Box

With Faux Faux Effects

This simple writing box, used for storing supplies as well as writing on, was enhanced with a fun finish I call "faux faux." While most faux finishes attempt to re-create expensive natural materials such as marble or hardwood, faux faux is pure fantasy. Its impact comes from your choice of colors and technique. Try borrowing ideas from the bright color combinations of old camp blankets to create some wonderful and outrageous effects. Use your imagination to

adapt any faux finish to create your own faux faux, such as a lavender marbled picture frame, or a gold and silver putty-grained dresser.

Tools and Materials

You will need artist's acrylic paints in terra cotta red and lettuce green; a 2" wide sponge brush; and a feather.

METHOD

To create this lovely little box I dragged a feather through a wet terra cotta wash to expose a soft lettuce green undercoat (as described in Project 45: Combed and Sponged Cabinet.). Working quickly, I dragged across the entire surface with an even action to make broad parallel lines.

52

Serving Tray

With Decoupage & Twig Handles

This 1950s picture frame made a perfect serving tray and with its flat sides it was an ideal foundation for twig work. To serve up some rustic charm, color photocopies of vintage post cards were decoupaged onto the tray's surface.

The latest technological advances in color copying machines and the abundance of pre-cut stickers are probably the two factors most responsible for the recent revival of the 17th-century art of decoupage. Once

known as *arte povero* or poor man's art, decoupage involves decorating surfaces with paper cutouts, which are then covered with a sealer so they leave an even surface. Decoupage is an inexpensive way to personalize and transform a host of flea market finds. With a bit of artistry, some scissors, glue and a few cutouts, you can transform anything from boxes to tables. Greeting cards, wrapping paper, magazines and family photographs are obvious sources for decoupage images, but for nostalgic pictures you will want to look at old cookbooks, children's books, catalogs, scrapbooks, song sheets, road maps, trading cards and the wealth of ephemera found at yard sales. Remember that you do not have to cut out the original. You can make a color copy of any image that appeals to you.

The most popular motifs in pre-cut stickers tend to be rosy-cheeked Victorian children, but there are also natural images such as birds, butterflies, pine cones and trees available that would be entirely appropriate for rustic cabin themes. Stickers can be purchased in many craft and stationery stores and through several mail order catalogs. Because they are pre-cut and pre-glued, stickers are quick and easy to apply; however, they are thicker than regular paper cutouts, and will require many more applications of sealer.

Tools and Materials

To remove prints and glass from old picture frames you will need a screwdriver for prying up nails on the back of old picture frames, as well as a pair of pliers for pulling the nails out. To decoupage you will need sharp scissors; images; multi-purpose white glue or decoupage medium (available at craft stores); sponge brushes; flat acrylic paint in whatever color you choose; and a matte acrylic sealer or flat urethane. (*Note:* A brayer or 1" wooden wallpaper roller, found at art supply and paint stores, is useful for smoothing down images and eliminating air bubbles, but your fingers will also work. If you have a roller, by all means

use it. Otherwise, I recommend that you wait until you have completed a few decoupage projects to decide if you need one.)

Making the Tray

METHOD

1. Remove the original print from your picture frame and replace it with a piece of plywood, cut to fit the frame.
2. Paint the entire tray with any good acrylic or latex paint. This turkey red color blended perfectly with the reddish brown hue of the willow branches.
3. Add twig handles to the two sides using wood screws.
4. Attach dry twigs to the edges of the tray with a glue gun. (*Note:* Always use dry twigs for glued projects. Fresh or green twigs will shrink as they dry and may pop off after they have been glued.)

Decoupage

1. Arrange the cutouts you have selected until you have a pleasing arrangement.
2. Use a sponge brush (or a finger) to apply glue to the back of one of the cutouts. (*Note:* If you are using white glue for the sealer coat, thin it a little with a few drops of water. There is no need to thin decoupage medium.) Lay your cutout or sticker down where you want it, pressing down firmly to remove any air bubbles. Repeat with all the remaining cutouts.
3. Allow to dry.
4. Apply a coat of sealer to the entire tray to protect the surface from spills and crumbs. Allow to dry and repeat sealer coat. Two or three sealer coats are usually enough to provide a surface that is smooth to the touch and not raised by your cutouts. It will take more coats of sealer to cover stickers.

53

Fire Board

Fake fireplaces were all the rage in the thirties and forties with apartment dwellers who yearned for houses and cabins containing the real thing. Now out of vogue, false fireplaces are often found at yard sales and auctions missing mantles, which have been removed to use as display shelves. This one, also stripped of its mantle, was only three dollars. It was the perfect foundation for a project I had long wanted to undertake—a fireboard.

178

Decorative summer fireboards were used to cheer dormant summer fireplaces and keep birds and small animals from getting into the house through the chimney. Early fireboards were often painted with *trompe l'oeil*, a French term meaning "to deceive the eye," and a style of painting in which objects are painted in realistic detail, often witty and usually decorative. These designs often show an urn of flowers with a surround of painted tiles. Sometimes simple red bricks were meticulously painted behind the flowers for a tongue-in-cheek depiction of the inside of the fireplace. Visit your local library to find books with pictures of antique fireboards for ideas and inspiration and then use your imagination to create your own rustic fireboard with stencils, decoupage or marbling.

For this fireboard, I photocopied birds from gift-wrapping and flowers from vintage hankies on a color photocopier, which I then cut out and decoupaged onto the board. (For detailed instructions on decoupage, see Project 52: Serving Tray With Decoupage.) The faux brick surround came with the fireboard and was left as is. Although my 20th-century fireplace has a damper so the chimney swallows and little creatures can't get in the house, this decorative fireboard is placed in front of the fireplace every summer.

54

Tool Box

With Crackled Finish

A country treasure like this tool carrier was simply too good to pass up, especially since it cost only six dollars at a winter auction. The carrier's simple shape and manageable size made it the perfect foundation for crackle work, where a top layer of paint separates from the under layer in random lines or cracks. As the demand for rustic cabin furnishings increases, so do the prices for naturally crackled antiques, as well as the expensive commercial counterfeits manufactured today.

A crackled finish can turn a plain piece of furniture into something special using this two-color technique.

Tools and Materials

You will need sandpaper; sponge brushes; acrylic paints; hide glue (available at woodworking shops and through woodworking catalogs); and clear acrylic sealer or polyurethane (optional).

METHOD

Crackling is best done on flat surfaces because the ingredients that make the paint crackle often run and drip. It is best to begin by crackling small pieces such as wooden boxes and picture frames, which are found in all shapes and sizes at yard sales. Experiment with scrap wood first.

Any existing paint need not be stripped but you will want to choose two colors for your project to achieve a contrasting look between the top and bottom paint layers. High-contrast colors such as red and green emphasize the crackled effect, while a subtle finish is achieved with related hues such as green and turquoise. To mimic an aged wood grain, use companion colors, such as light brown and buff, or tan and khaki. The base coat will be the color of the cracks and the top coat will be the main color of the piece.

1. If necessary, wash your project with warm water to remove any surface dirt.
2. Lightly sand the piece to remove any loose paint.
3. On unfinished wood, apply a primer coat and allow it to dry for 3 to 6 hours.
4. Using the sponge brush, apply the base coat of paint and allow it to dry for 3 to 4 hours.
5. Apply a second base coat and allow it to dry for 24 hours. It is essential that the base coat is dry before you add the crackle coat, so make sure to allow enough drying time.
6. Mix one part water with two parts room-temperature hide

glue in a small container. Using a sponge brush, apply a generous amount of glue onto the surface using smooth, even strokes.

7. Check to make sure the glue has completely covered all the surfaces before beginning the crackle coat. If the surface is porous, sometimes the glue/water mixture soaks through the top surface and therefore cannot do its job of causing the top layer to separate from the bottom layer of paint. If the glue has soaked through in some areas, reapply another layer of the glue/water and allow that to dry to the touch, which should take approximately 30 minutes. *Note:* The hide glue should not be totally dry at this point.

8. Working quickly, using even strokes, apply a top coat of paint with a sponge brush. *Note:* It is very important not to overlap the strokes as this will prevent the paint from crackling. Crackling should appear almost immediately. Do not be tempted to go over the paint after it has already crackled. Allow the piece to dry thoroughly, usually 24 to 38 hours.

9. Use a tinted wash to further enhance the aged appearance of the finished piece. Use a sponge or a brush to apply a weak solution of watery brown wash (see "dirty water wash", in Project 3: One Drawer Stand With a Twig Drawer & Antiquing), pressing the dark color into the cracks.

10. Once the piece has dried, you can apply one or more coats of polyurethane varnish or acrylic sealer to protect the finish.

PART 4

Recycling to Achieve the Rustic Look

RECYCLED RUSTICS

Recycling is nothing new. Our grandparents saved everything. Paper envelopes were cut and stacked to be used for making lists and leaving notes for the milkman; pieces of string were kept and formed into a ball and left in a string holder, waiting to be reused. Tea tins were used to store nuts and bolts in the workshop and old carpets were used to re-cover footstools and repair valises. In the fifties books were published to instruct housewives how to make compote bowls out of angel food cake pans and Jell-O molds. Mid-century house decorating magazines included articles encouraging readers to transform attic junk into desirable "decorator pieces" inexpensively. Most of these project instructions were for accessories, called variously centerpieces, decorative arrangements, kitchen brighteners and conversation pieces. In the late sixties a handful of designers celebrated the beauty of manufactured items, turning tin cans into pop art tables and Styrofoam packaging into wall art.

Now it seems that everyone is fascinated with recycling to capture individual style. Garage sale items and simple techniques join to make this kind of decorating fun and worthwhile. A lively mix of collectibles and hand-crafted objects come together to create the timeless charm of America's rustic style.

55

Pillows

With Tobacco Flags & Pennants

As playful as they are useful, these pillows are what rustic cabin decorating is all about. Ordinary souvenir pennants are plentiful at flea markets and make wonderful pillows as well as framed wall art. Collectible pennants, such as those that date political or circus events, will probably continue to increase in value and should not be used to make pillows. They can be framed but must be kept out of the sunlight.

Tobacco flags were given away with tobacco purchases at the turn

of the century and when they show up at sales today, they usually cost only a dollar or so. If a dealer has a bundle of flags you may be able to get a special price on the whole lot. These flags came in a stack of one hundred for only ten cents apiece and the gentleman who sold them to me was happy to get rid of them. He told me they had been cluttering up his bureau drawers for too many years. Be on the lookout for these little treasures, for their vivid colors will add color and eye-catching style to any room.

These simple pillows can be assembled by hand sewing or with a sewing machine.

Tools and Materials

Pennant Pillow

You will need three vintage pennants; two pieces of red felt 22" by 30"; 1½ yards of heavy-duty fusible web (available at sewing centers); red sewing thread; pinking shears (available at sewing centers and craft stores); an electric iron; a pillow form or stuffing.

Tobacco Flag Pillow

You will need six assorted vintage flags (*Note:* Other vintage textiles may be substituted, such as printed napkins or drapery fabric); two pieces of teal felt, 21" by 21"; ¾ yard heavy-duty fusible web; teal thread; scissors; an electric iron; and a 16" square pillow form or stuffing.

Pennant Pillow

METHOD

1. To begin, arrange the pennants on top of a piece of red felt, allowing for a 2" border around the pennants. Pin in place. Cut the felt to size before you attach the pennants to avoid any mistakes, because once the pennants have been bonded onto the felt, they cannot be removed.
2. Cut the red felt with pinking shears.

3. Cut another piece of red felt with pinking shears for the backing, the same size as the piece in step 1.

4. Cut a piece of the web to fit the backs of the pennants, taking care not to allow any web to extend beyond the pennant or a sticky residue will show on the finished pillow.

5. Following the manufacturer's directions, and working with one at a time, fuse a pennant to the felt. (*Note:* Felt never unravels and doesn't require hemming.)

6. Pin the scalloped edged backing in place.

7. Top stitch the front to the back along the edges of the pennants, leaving an opening along one edge to insert the stuffing.

8. Stuff the pillow and sew the opening closed.

Tobacco Flag Pillow

1. Read the directions above for the Pennant Pillow.

2. Center the flags on the 21" felt square. Pin in place.

3. Following the manufacturer's directions, fuse the flags to the felt.

4. Pin the backing in place.

5. Stitch the pillow front to the backing, by stitching around the edges of the flags, leaving an opening along one edge to insert the stuffing.

6. Insert the pillow stuffing and sew the opening closed.

56

Tobacco Felt

Within a Frame

Framed in a wonderful garage sale pine frame, these tobacco felts are used like graphics to create original and imaginative art. Depending on the depth of your frame, you may choose to use a piece of cardboard or foam core for additional backing. This added backing should be used to help keep the flags from slipping around under the glass.

Tools and Materials

To protect and preserve your treasures, you will want to use acid-free framing materials, available at art shops, photo stores and some craft shops; conservation glass (available from glass and mirror shops) to protect the fabrics from fading, cut to fit your frame; archival-quality matte board; nontoxic, removable adhesive (or archival glue); white household glue; brown kraft paper; wire brads or framing points; a picture wire and hooks (long enough to span the back of your frame). You will also need a small hammer and a utility knife to cut your matte board.

METHOD

1. Cut the matte board to size.
2. Arrange the felts on the matte board until you are satisfied with their placement.
3. Use nontoxic, removable adhesive (or archival glue) to adhere the felts to the matte board.
4. Place the assembly under the conservation glass in the frame.
5. If using additional backing, cut the cardboard or foam core to fit and place it on the matte board.
6. Hammer wire brads or framing points sideways around the inside perimeter of the frame to keep everything firmly in place.
7. For a professional finish, run a bead of white household glue around the back of the frame and place a piece of brown kraft paper, cut to size, over the glue.
8. When the glue is dry, and the kraft paper is in place, complete the project by attaching picture wire onto the back of the frame.

57

Serving Tray

With Twig Handles

Crafted from the top of a discarded wooden cheese box and two flexible branches, this rustic serving tray is designed to resist tipping. Inspired by an ancient Turkish design and reinvented with twigs, this marvelous serving tray permits you to serve a trayload of beverages with one hand.

Tools and Materials

You will need a wooden cheese box or box top, approximately 16"

in diameter and 1" deep. Brie cheese still comes packed in these boxes and cheese shops or deli counters in large supermarkets will often give them away. You will also need two pliable willow branches 30" long and ¼" to ½" in diameter for handles; a 5" long, ½" diameter branch for the carry rod and four wood screws. A 20" long piece of rawhide is tied to the rod and the handles. A hiking boot lace works nicely for this purpose.

METHOD

1. Drill four evenly spaced holes along the circumference of the tray.
2. Carefully bend a handle part into an arc shape.
3. Place the handle ends over two opposite pre-drilled holes, and attach from the bottom with wood screws.
4. Repeat with the remaining handle part.
5. Attach the carry rod to the top center of the handles, using the rawhide to make a series of square knots.

58

Hassock

With Persian Carpet Upholstery

A torn and tattered ten-dollar green vinyl box is hidden beneath this handsome upholstered hassock which looks at once rich and rustic. Used, handwoven oriental rugs can be found reasonably priced at sales and auctions when they are ripped and worn. Even the smallest remnant is worth buying to use for upholstery, pillows or even framing. These time-worn orphans are usually not salable, except to

those who realize that a handwoven rug is a truly won-drous thing, and well worth taking the time to preserve for its bold patterns and earthen colors.

Tools and Materials

Once you have enough rug scraps to cover your box, the only additional tools required will be a pair of scissors, a heavy-duty staple gun, and white household glue.

METHOD

1. Cut a piece of the carpet to fit around the sides of the box plus 1".
2. Cut a width to fit the height of the box plus 2" to go under the base and another 2" for attaching to the top rim. (*Note:* If the lid is hinged, remove the hinges and install them after the upholstering is complete.)
3. Measure and cut a length of carpet to fit over the lid's front, back and two sides, allowing approximately 2" extra to go under the lid.
4. Starting at a back corner, wrap the carpet around the box with about a 1" excess along the long edge, and 2" extending on the bottom and top. Use glue to attach the overlapped side edge, and temporarily pin in place until the glue dries.
5. Use the staple gun to attach the carpet under the box.
6. Fold the corners like a package and staple in place.
7. Cut the corners at the top of the box to help them fold up inside and use a staple gun to attach the carpet to the top edge in the same manner.
8. Glue the carpet to the front lid edge.
9. Cover the lid with carpet, wrapping edges around the front, back and sides, package style. Staple the edges under the lid.

FIG. 58-1

59

Footstool

With Persian Carpet Upholstery

Covered with a scrap of very worn rug and trimmed with a marvelous piece of patterned trim, this versatile ottoman provides additional seating or will serve as an end table. A walnut polyurethane gel stain and gilding were used on the legs. (See Staining in Project 47: Coffee Table With Faux Leather Finish, Staining & Gilding).

The original upholstery was very clean and required only a swish of fabric shampoo and vacuum cleaning before it was covered. The rug was simple to attach. It was cut to size and hand sewn in place to the existing upholstery with heavy-duty thread and a curved upholstery needle. The trim was attached in the same fashion.

60 Chair

With Rag Weaving

I don't know why there are so many chairs around at sales and auctions, but there always seems to be a selection to choose from. Most people get rid of chairs with missing seats, but it is a simple matter to revitalize and update any open-seat chair with rag weaving. A kitchen table surrounded with a collection of mismatched rag-woven chairs looks wonderfully folksy and homey.

198

Tools and Materials

Any number of open-seat or open-back chairs are suitable for rag weaving, including platform rockers and folding wooden beach chairs. Assorted cotton or wool fabrics that can be torn into strips are used for weaving. A needle and heavy-duty thread, along with a hammer and nail (or staple gun), are optional tools. Read all the directions before you begin.

The rag strips can be made from printed calicos or from medium-weight, firmly woven wool. When choosing fabrics, concentrate on color rather than motifs to reflect your taste. Patterned fabrics, such as plaids, tweeds and checks, create interesting textures when combined. You can mix different fabrics, but generally it is best to work with fabrics of the same weight. The strips of 1940s florals used here capture the essence of rustic cabin charm.

METHOD

1. Begin by tearing fabric into ½" or 1" wide strips. Lengths vary, depending on supply. A good working length is six to nine feet. If your fabric will not produce lengths this long, join additional strips to make the lengths by knotting or sewing the ends of the strips together, so they form one long continuous strip. Additional lengths can be added by knotting or sewing as the work proceeds. I like to wrap and form the strips into a workable ball, like a ball of yarn for knitting.

2. To start weaving, tie, nail or staple one end of the fabric strip to the back stretcher and wrap the strip over and around the front stretcher. Continue wrapping from back to front over the stretchers. Tie, nail or staple the end in place on the back stretcher as you did to begin.

FIG. 60-1

FIG. 60-2

3. When the front-to-back wrapping is complete, the under-over (side-to-side) weaving begins. Fasten one end of the fabric strip along the corner of a side stretcher. The seat is created by weaving under and over both the upper and lower initial layer of wrapped strips, creating a flat surface. (*Note:* If you are knotting, rather than sewing the ends together, keep the knots on the underside to create a smooth seat.)

4. End the weaving by attaching the end of the strip to the side stretcher.

61
Table

From a Cedar Door With Log Legs

When we removed the Bilko doors from our house in order to build an outdoor porch, we saved the silvery gray wooden doors to make a picnic table to use on the porch. It was a case of recycling at its best. The weathered table suits the porch beautifully and nothing was wasted.

Tools and Materials

You will need a single-bit axe for felling trees; a crosscut handsaw; a

ruler; a marking pencil; a ⅜" variable speed drill and drill bits; drywall screws; a miter box and miter box saw (*Note:* A lap joint can be substituted for a mitered joint if want to simplify your table (see Figure 61-3); safety goggles and work gloves; a level; a wood door 87" × 34"; four cedar logs, 4" in diameter and 27" long, for the table legs. (*Note:* Because the logs may require trimming to ensure a straight table after they are installed, it is a good idea to begin with logs that are longer than the desired finished length.) You will also need two 30" long, 2" by 10" fir boards for joining the legs to the table; and four 1½" cedar strips, 87" and 34" long, for the apron.

FIG. 61-1

1. Using the drill and drywall screws, attach one 2" by 10" fir board to two cedar logs. This method of attaching the logs helps to make your table strong and straight without the need for additional braces. Repeat with the remaining two legs.
2. Turn the table top, top side down, onto your work surface.
3. Position a board/leg structure, one at a time, to each corner, at a location 2" from the edge with four drywall screws.
4. Stand the table upright and use a level to make sure that the table surface is perfectly horizontal.
5. To add the table apron, measure and cut the cedar strips to length.
6. Attach the apron parts to the underside table edge using drywall screws.

There is something reminiscent of cabin picnics and family feasts when you gather around this door-table. For the look and feel of a wonderful vintage table, leave the silvery gray finish unsealed.

METHOD

FIG. 61-2

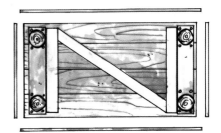

FIG. 61-3

62

Chair

With Suede Skirt Upholstery

Some of the furnishings we most admire are the result of small budgets and a good dose of imagination. When it comes to thrift, I often think of going with my grandmother to visit the seamstress when I was a child. This was an annual summer ritual. On these occasions my grandmother and I were always served fresh lemonade and coconut cookies in the little room adjacent to the sewing room. I remember most fondly of all the flowered chintz pillows that graced the chairs on which we sat. They were backed with snips of leather and suede salvaged from worn jackets and handbags. When I found this sturdy chair for only eight dollars, I decided to try my hand at remnant leather upholstery. It took some searching to find suitable leather scraps to refinish the chair. When the local thrift store had its annual spring half-price sale I found two suede skirts for five dollars each. They provided more than enough material to reupholster the chair and create a true original.

About Upholstering

*S*ome upholstering jobs require more skill and knowledge than this simple chair. If the chair you want to upholster has a sagging seat, turn it over to try and determine the problem. Sometimes the problem is simply that the webbing has come loose, in which case it can easily be tacked back into place. If, on the other hand, your chair suffers from loose springs or missing stuffing, the springs will have to be retied and the seat restuffed before you can reupholster. For more detailed information on upholstering, consult your local library for books on the subject.

Tools and Materials

You will need a hammer with a claw for removing tacks; large scissors; a measuring tape; upholsterer's size tacks; decorative upholstery nails (these come in a variety of finishes or can be painted to suit your project); enough suede or leather to cover the chair, a pencil, a measuring tape and stuffing for the seat (if necessary).

METHOD

1. Carefully remove the old upholstery fabric in one piece, if possible. You will want to use the old fabric as a pattern to cut your new seat and back.
2. Once the old piece has been removed, adjust the stuffing or padding as necessary. You may be able to separate lumps of old stuffing and fluff them up with your fingers. Add new cotton padding, available at sewing centers, if the foundation padding is worn.

3. It is a good idea to stretch and tack a clean piece of muslin over old (or new) padding to guarantee a smooth seat. Cut the muslin to size. Turn under the raw edges. Tack in place with #2 tacks.

4. Cut the suede or leather to size, discarding buttons or zippers. You may have to sew several pieces together to get enough to cover the seat. Suede or leather skirt pieces can be sewn together on a home sewing machine or by hand with the appropriate needles, which you can find at your local fabric store.

5. Arrange the material over the seat and/or back, taking care to center any seams. Using a pencil and measuring tape, mark dots approximately 1" apart for the upholstery nails. (*Note:* The raw edge of the suede is tucked under as you proceed.)

6. Beginning at the back of the seat, in the center, place the first upholstery nail and tap into place. Continue nailing along the back, to the right and left of the center, about one-third of the way, pulling the suede taut as you go, always tucking the raw edge under.

7. Repeat nailing on the front edge in the same manner as the back. Begin at the center and work to the right and the left (toward the corners) one-third of the way, keeping the fabric taut.

8. The sides are attached in the same manner. Begin at the center and work to the right and the left, toward the corners, one-third of the way, keeping the fabric taut. Remember to fold the edges under as you proceed.

9. Tuck the edges under and complete the corners last.

10. The back of the chair is upholstered in the same manner as the seat. Always begin at the center. Work from back to front or top to bottom, one-third of the way, pulling the fabric taut, then the sides from the center, right and left. Finish with the corners.

Note: A gimp or decorative braid may be used to trim the edges of the fabric before the upholstery nails are tapped in place. White household glue or fabric glue is used for attaching a gimp. Be on the lookout at flea markets and yard sales for unusual trimmings. New gimps and braids, as well as ribbons and bindings, are available at sewing centers and trimming stores.